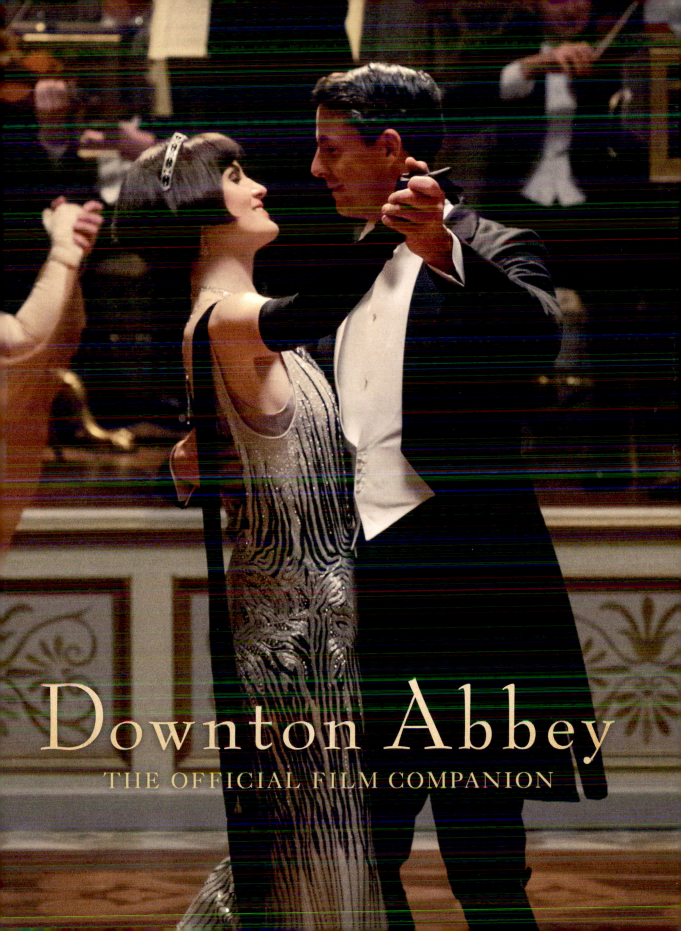

Downton Abbey

THE OFFICIAL FILM COMPANION

Downton Abbey

THE OFFICIAL FILM COMPANION

EMMA MARRIOTT

FOREWORD BY JULIAN FELLOWES

ST. MARTIN'S PRESS
NEW YORK

CONTENTS

FOREWORD

It seems strange to write it now but when, a decade ago, Gareth Neame suggested that I might like to create the series that later became *Downton Abbey*, I wasn't all that enthusiastic. Some years before, I had written a film called *Gosford Park*, examining the lives of a group of house guests, and their servants, at a shooting party in 1932, and Gareth's idea was that I should revisit the same territory, only this time for television. At first, it seemed like asking for a second slice of cake, and anyway, the underlying message of the film had been that this kind of life was coming to an end for all but a minuscule minority. But the last problem was solved by moving the starting point back by twenty years, from 1932 to 1912, and soon I found myself considering issues that interested me but had never before found an outlet in my work.

What was it like for that tidal wave of American heiresses who came to the rescue of the British aristocracy in the 1890s and 1900s after twenty or thirty years, separated as they were from the values of the New World? How would it be for a man to inherit a position and an estate when they had grown up in an entirely different way? I had a friend who arrived on these shores as the heir to a great name when he had started life in a different culture entirely. Could he make a success of it? In real life, as far as my friend was concerned, the answer was yes and he did, very much so, but how would it be for Matthew Crawley?

And so gradually, as often happens when you start to work on a new project, I was dragged into the lives of these people I had made up but came to love, until they formed the centre of my world, and to my great pleasure, it soon became apparent that they would bring a lot of enjoyment to people almost everywhere.

Being caught up in a phenomenon is hard to describe. It was unbelievable at first, but rewarding too and a real sign that, just for once, we had got it right. As it happens, I have been lucky over the years, but when I die, I am fairly certain that *Downton Abbey* will be the marker of my passing. Nor do I resent this. Any more than, I am sure, Matthew Wiener would mind being remembered for *Mad Men* or Aaron Sorkin for *The West Wing*. I enjoyed the initial challenge of finding an audience for the show, and the renewed thrown gauntlet at the start of every season of proving we could keep up the standard we had set. I think we did, although it sounds vain to say it. Our audiences stayed loyal until the finish, and now we have the pleasure of giving them the chance of another visit to that wonderful house (for Highclere Castle *is* a wonderful house) and the fun of catching up with their favourite characters. Actually, there was something almost surreal, like a kind of time travel, as we gathered together at the read-through, and then reassembled in the great hall, the cast back in costume, the crew resuming their tasks. Now it is done and we are ready to show the film to the public in the hope of their approval.

This book will allow them to share the fun of making the movie, the different stages of development, the various departments involved. It is about our return to Downton, and I hope it will have a favoured place on the shelves of those who buy it, as a lasting memento of a show that found a way into their hearts.

Julian Fellowes
June 2019

The year is 1927. Downton Abbey, the seat of Lord Grantham, is cloaked in morning mist, just before the sun breaks through and rises steadily over the Yorkshire countryside.

Inside, the servants are up and ready for the day: Mr Barrow is in his butler's livery, Mrs Patmore and Daisy are busy in the kitchen, Mrs Hughes attends to her paperwork. Upstairs, Lady Mary and Tom Branson are already in the dining room; Lord Grantham is making his way down. All is as it should be and has always been – a normal day on the Downton estate.

Yet for the previous few hours, a letter has been journeying towards the house. Beginning its passage in a gilded room, it is placed inside a leather satchel and carried away by a liveried official. Mailbags are loaded on to a night train, and as it thunders through the darkness, postal workers sort letters into pigeonholes. At dawn, a van winds its way through the waking Downton village until it stops at the post office. It's a GPO motorcycle that drives up the gravelled approach to Downton Abbey and stops outside the servants' entrance – a sign of the changing times. Andy the footman opens the back door and the postman holds up the letter.

The letter bears the crest of the royal coat of arms, its journey having begun at Buckingham Palace. It announces the impending arrival of King George and Queen Mary, who are to visit Downton Abbey as part of their tour of Yorkshire. Almost at once the familiar rhythm of the house is altered – the day, and the next few weeks, will be anything but normal.

DOWNTON REVISITED

GARETH NEAME

Producer

Over a decade ago, Gareth Neame had a seed of an idea. With over twenty-five years' experience working in British drama, he probably had a great many ideas in his head. This particular one, however, would lead to the creation of one of the most successful television dramas ever made, capturing millions of fans across the world, in over 250 territories, earning critical acclaim and recognition including three Golden Globes, fifteen Emmys, a BAFTA Television Special Award and four Screen Actors Guild awards.

Gareth had for a long time thought that the setting of an English country estate could provide the perfect backdrop for a television series. Some years earlier, he had seen Robert Altman's film *Gosford Park* and had been impressed by its compelling depiction of country-house life, both those working in the house and its guests. He discussed the idea with Julian Fellowes, who had won an Academy Award for his original screenplay for *Gosford Park*. Drilling into the concept further, Gareth and Julian agreed the television show should have an Edwardian setting, but with a pace of narrative and density of stories more familiar to contemporary dramas. Crucially,

it should follow the lives of the family and their servants in equal measure.

Some days later, Julian emailed to Gareth his initial thoughts on the many characters who would come to inhabit their imagined estate. Above stairs, there was the Earl and his American wife; below, the butler and housekeeper. These characters almost leapt off the page, as if Fellowes had lived with them for many years. The world he created instantly came alive, and *Downton Abbey* was born.

The decision to make a *Downton Abbey* film was not quite so instantaneous, but gradually gained traction as the phenomenal success of the television series grew.

'There was never an exact moment of "let's make a *Downton* movie"', explains Gareth, 'but we had been thinking about it at around the end of season four and by the time we were halfway through shooting the final season, Julian and I were already getting into the detail of what the film could be.

'Some people felt we finished a little prematurely in season six and I think we could have gone on for another year. NBCUniversal, our

the storyline, to devise a plot that was very much *Downton* in feel but which would work on the big screen. 'Julian came up with the idea of the royal visit,' explains Gareth, 'which appealed because it gave the characters this once-in-a-lifetime event, the "jewel in the crown" if you like. *Downton* often has a myriad of storylines but the royal visit provides a shared endeavour that all the characters are involved in. We see them on the back foot, usurped by people who think they are better than them, and we see our heroes fight back.'

With an agreed storyline for the film in place, Julian set to work on the script. Continuing the close working practice developed during the making of the television series, Julian provided the first draft of the script, which Gareth then went through, making notes. As always, these early stages of the script development were an intimate and very focused process, involving just Julian, Gareth and fellow producer Liz Trubridge, as they went over draft after draft of the script until they were happy with it.

A clear challenge for the creative team was to make the multiple storylines of the large ensemble cast of *Downton Abbey* suitable for a movie, which usually has just one or a handful of characters involved in one story. 'We worked really hard to give each of them a story and Julian is brilliant at juggling a large number of characters, all of them strongly defined with their own narrative,' explains Gareth. 'The audience want to see their favourite character do something meaningful, plus I had to get all these actors to commit to the film, so they needed a reason to be there!'

When they were all satisfied with the script, the team then sent it to Focus Features, who were

One of the first people Gareth and Liz Trubridge recruited to the team was director Michael Engler, who they had worked with on a few episodes of the television series. As Liz says: 'The joy of working with Michael is that he is so collaborative – you can question things with him and he seeks to know what you think – and he has the most infectious enthusiasm for the project. He also works incredibly hard and he's so experienced that he knows exactly what he wants and if something on the day goes wrong he is very capable of adapting.'

parent company, were interested to see if a *Downton* movie could happen, and during the filming of the final season, Julian and I said we wanted to do a movie. I really felt I had a duty to the fans and if we hadn't got it off the ground, I would have felt that we had failed them. I think the knowledge that we were developing a film has sustained many people for the past three years.'

Once the will was there to do a movie, the first key step was to establish the main premise of funding and distributing the film. Gareth's role as producer is multi-layered and involves procuring finance for projects as well as running Carnival Films, collaborating on scripts and approving casting, editing and post-production. Once the script had the definite go-ahead from Focus, Carnival were then able to send it to the cast.

For a movie, *Downton Abbey* has an unusually large cast and while the original twenty actors were keen in principle, getting them all together in one place for filming proved a real challenge. None could be recast and all had busy schedules, meaning that there was little room for manoeuvre when dates for filming were finally agreed.

Along with securing the returning members of the cast, Gareth and his team also needed to find new cast members, some of whom were playing real people from the past. These included King George V and Queen Mary, along with their daughter, Princess Mary, and her husband, Lord Lascelles. The royal family had previously made an appearance in the final episode of season four, in which the Crawley family managed to stop a compromising love letter from the Prince of Wales to his mistress, Freda Dudley Ward, getting into the wrong hands. 'It is fun to have the fictional characters of *Downton* merging with the real world, as we do in the movie,' explains Gareth. 'It is said that Princess Mary had an unhappy marriage but she ultimately saw it through, and we enjoyed playing with the concept that Branson gave her the advice she needed, that our imaginary creations helped make the marriage work.'

In finding new cast members, not only did the team want to find the right actors but, for those playing the royals, they were also keen to find

Producer Liz Trubridge is not only involved with the script and development of the movie but also works closely with director Michael Engler and co-producer Mark Hubbard during the shoot. A typical day involves getting to the set very early in the morning to check that everything is okay. 'We'll talk through the day, what we need to achieve and where we'll need to spend the most amount of time. The job of a producer is really an enabler, to make sure everyone can do the best work they're capable of.'

people who could resemble them physically. Casting director Jill Trevellick oversaw the process and certainly Simon Jones and Geraldine James provided good likenesses of the King and the Queen, especially once costume and make-up had worked their magic.

While most of the new cast were approached by Jill through official channels, Academy-nominated Imelda Staunton, who is married to Jim Carter (Mr Carson), was by association already very much part of the family. Nonetheless, doing a film version of *Downton* enabled Jill to approach actors of the stature of Imelda, who plays the role of Lady Bagshaw to perfection.

While the team had for some years wanted David Haig to appear in *Downton*, the logistics never worked out. Fate, however, was to play its part when in 2017 Gareth bumped into David at a fish restaurant in Dorset. 'I hadn't worked with him for a very long time, but I mentioned that we had a good role in a film he might be interested in – two months later, he's signed up for the role of Mr Wilson [the King's Page of the Backstairs], and it's fantastic to have him on board.'

The arrival of new cast members also brought in new love interests for the *Downton* characters, in the form of the King's valet Mr Ellis and Mr Barrow; and Lady Bagshaw's maid, Lucy, who catches the eye of Tom Branson. Romance has always been a key element in *Downton Abbey*, driven often by Mary and Edith's pursuit of it. 'In the final season, both of the sisters had found happiness,' adds Gareth, 'so Branson was the one central younger character who hadn't found lasting love since losing his wife, so it was great for him to find it at last, or so we hope.'

In taking *Downton Abbey* to the big screen, the production team also had the task of giving the show more of a cinematic feel, which is no mean feat when the series already had the highest of production values on television. In recreating the style and etiquette of another age, the makers of *Downton Abbey* had always been detailed and unrelenting in their work, creating a show that was as much a visual treat as it was an entertaining drama. 'We knew the film had to give the fans what they wanted, and it also had to be something more. The look of the film – set pieces, costumes, locations, cinematography – had to be another twenty-five to fifty per cent on top. We wanted it to feel like the show, but bigger and better, and more polished.'

To achieve this, Gareth and Liz brought in the key 'architects' of *Downton* – director Michael Engler, production designer Donal Woods and costume designer Anna Robbins – all of whom had worked on the television series. 'We wanted continuity for the sets and costumes,' explains Gareth, 'but we also wanted to introduce some fresh components and for that reason chose to use a cinematographer who was entirely new to *Downton*, and so the very talented Ben Smithard joined the team as DOP [director of photography].'

While the film returns to Highclere, it also features some beautiful new locations as well as colourful set pieces involving hundreds of actors (and horses), all of which add further spectacle and scale to the film. These include the very grand Harewood House in Yorkshire, and the ballroom of Wentworth Woodhouse, which is captured in all its glory in one of the final scenes of the film.

Journeying from that first spark of an idea that was inspired by a movie, it is somehow fitting that the show is now to make its own transition to the big screen. It's a thought that has, of course, occurred to Gareth as he's looked back at the incredible journey that *Downton Abbey* has taken him on over the last few years. 'It's circular in a way, and when we were shooting on set the other day, I did joke to the actors, "This is good, I think we should make a TV show out of it."'

'We wanted it to feel like the show, but bigger and better, and more polished.'

Gareth Neame,
producer

'Julian is brilliant at juggling a large number of characters, all of them strongly defined with their own narrative.'

Gareth Neame,
producer

JULIAN FELLOWES

Writer and Producer

It is incredible to think that Downton Abbey and all the people who live and work in the great country estate of Lord and Lady Grantham are the imaginings of Julian Fellowes. Without him, Violet, the Dowager Countess, the Crawley sisters, Carson, Anna and Daisy would not exist – one can hardly believe it, as they seem so real. Their loves, lives, deep sorrows and great joys have all been conjured in his mind, before being brought to life by the actors who play them and the production team who build and shape their world.

Over the last few years, Julian's splendid scripts have followed the lives of some thirty or so key characters over six seasons, with equal weight given to the family upstairs and those working for them, with storylines that twist and intertwine, enthralling millions of viewers in the process. His characters are well-defined and entirely credible, they make mistakes and sometimes reveal surprising sides to their personalities, and the lives of the servant household are just as complex and messy as that of the Crawleys.

The world in which *Downton Abbey* is set is also one that Fellowes knows something about, having witnessed the tail end of its heyday. As

a boy, he wandered around the forlorn country estates of family friends or relatives, and glimpsed the last few debutantes dressed in white curtseying at Grosvenor House. It was of course a vanishing world, but he, like many of us, is fascinated by the rules and rituals that governed the lives of people in the Edwardian and interwar period, even while so much around them was changing.

The film is set squarely in this febrile world: it is 1927 and all around there is change – cars, not carriages, are the norm; Edith and Mary want to be firmly in control of their own lives; and Daisy yearns for more than a life of service – but the Crawleys are still at the helm of Downton Abbey and the estate is largely intact.

The arrival of the King and Queen of course throws everything into disarray, a pivotal event that Julian and producer Gareth Neame thought could work well in the film. 'I felt we needed an event that would affect the upstairs and downstairs community, all of them involved in the same endeavour to give the film unity,' explains Julian. 'In a television series, stories are often not resolved within one week, many go through three or four episodes or even seasons, and there are lots of variations with the stories. For a film, every story must on the whole have its resolution, whether it's unhappy or happy.'

The concept of the royal visit also appealed to Julian because, like all the stories in *Downton Abbey*, it is underpinned by historical reality. In the 1920s, King George V and Queen Mary regularly toured the UK, and stayed at the houses of local peers just as they do in the film. 'It's all quite believable that they would tour Yorkshire,' adds Julian, 'and it's remarkable what they would bring with them. I read one royal used to bring his own furniture, which I thought might be a step too far for the film, but I liked the idea that the house in effect becomes theirs while they're in it. And by bringing in their servant household, as happened in reality and at Downton, it would be as disruptive for the staff as much as anyone else.'

Julian also remembers his grandparents talking about being summoned to meet the Duke and Duchess of York at a nearby house party just before they became king and queen. 'The 1920s was a sensitive period for the crown, the First World War had swept away many of the great thrones of Europe,' he adds. 'Everyone needed to be sure that the monarchy had a role, and its value needed to be reaffirmed with the people. In fact, King George and Queen Mary were pretty successful at doing this, so much so that the monarchy was able to weather the crisis of their son's later abdication.

'So part of all that was getting out there and not just meeting the local toffs and waltzing but also being seen by the local population, who could see you were real and not just a profile on a stamp. As part of a visit they would organise a public

event, just like the parade we have in the village, so the public could have a legitimate excuse to come and see them.'

Like the rest of the production team, Julian was keen that the actors playing the royal couple should be good likenesses. He also didn't want the portrayal of Queen Mary to be overly stuffy, as his feeling was that she was more than her very formal public persona. 'She knew very well that when the public saw them, they would see what they wanted to see – a proper king and a proper queen, and she had this imperative not to be disappointing. But she was interested in all sorts of things, had friends who were writers and in the theatre, and she was probably more fun to be around than we might think. The formality she gave off acted perhaps as a kind of protection or a shield, to cope with the pressures of being a royal.'

The seemingly unhappy marriage between Princess Mary and her husband, Lord Lascelles, is also woven into the storyline, a union that did seem something of a mismatch. 'At the time, there were so many defunct royal houses abroad that Princess Mary had to marry domestically,' explains Julian, 'and there were a limited number of senior noblemen who had big enough estates and a way of life that was appropriate for the only daughter of the King. I think the list was pretty short.'

The film also includes Imelda Staunton's portrayal of the Queen's lady-in-waiting Maud Bagshaw. The character is entirely fictitious, although her predicament is not. We discover she has had an illegitimate child – as of course happened in high society, which could just about turn a blind eye to affairs after marriage but was totally unforgiving of illegitimacy. 'Each class had to develop ways of dealing with this kind of situation,' adds Julian. 'Lady Bagshaw chose to keep her daughter Lucy close by and in doing so has to reduce her social status to throw people off the scent.'

Maud Bagshaw adds to the plethora of strong female characters that have always featured in *Downton Abbey*, and in the movie, both Lady Mary and Anna Bates show their mettle in their respective spheres of the house. Julian is also adept at giving older women, who are often overlooked on the big and small screen, their due prominence. Principal of these of course is Violet, Dowager Countess of Grantham, played by Maggie Smith, who delivers some of the most delicious bon mots in the show. It's almost as if there's a particular chemistry between the two, Julian clearly writing her part with real affection and Maggie delivering her lines perfectly. Julian modelled Violet on his own Great-aunt Isie, who was born in 1880 and lived through extraordinary times until 1971. These redoubtable women were (and probably still are) common to all families, as Julian has said: 'There was a whole generation of women like Violet . . . these incredibly frightening matriarchs in all sorts of family situations, that everyone was half-terrified of and half-loved.'

As queen of the zinger and withering put-down, Violet also brings plenty of humour to the show, as do other characters, with comedy a constant thread in the series. Julian also ensures the film has its share of laugh-out-loud moments, not least the scene when Mr Molesley (played by Kevin Doyle) serves the King and Queen at dinner. Just when everyone is trying to be very proper in front of the royal couple, Molesley makes the most horrendous

faux pas by addressing the King directly – perhaps not a huge deal in today's world, but we really do feel his total mortification afterwards.

Romance is also deftly woven into the drama – we've seen the slow burn of attraction and the welling of emotion for characters young and old, even Isobel, who in season six was allowed her own fairytale ending with marriage to Lord Merton. In the film it's the turn of Tom Branson and also Mr Barrow, both of whom have had their fair share of sorrow and who viewers feel deserve happiness and love.

That search for happiness is very much at the core of *Downton Abbey*; there are dark and sad stories, but there's always an overwhelming feeling of positivity. 'Julian isn't ashamed of that,' says producer Gareth Neame. 'He wants to make people happy, he wants people to enjoy themselves, and I think he's remarkable at what he can do.'

RETURN TO HIGHCLERE

Making the movie of *Downton Abbey* meant of course returning to Highclere Castle, the key location for filming and the setting for Lord and Lady Grantham's family estate. The castle, with its soaring towers and grand facade, is a powerful symbol of an aristocratic past, befitting of a family just like the Crawleys, who have for generations built and nurtured the house and its estate.

Highclere Castle, a commanding presence in the Hampshire countryside, has its own illustrious history and has been lived in by several generations of the Carnarvon family. Remodelled in 'high Elizabethan style' between 1839 and 1842, the similarity of Highclere to the Houses of Parliament in London is no coincidence – both buildings are the work of the architect Sir Charles Barry. Despite its grand proportions, Highclere has an intimate and characterful feel inside. The castle, however, is not just a museum piece but a real home, currently to the 8th Earl and Countess of Carnarvon who, despite the disruption caused by filming, have always delighted in the close relationship they have built up over the years with the cast and crew of *Downton Abbey*.

Inside the house, filming takes place in the impressive great hall, staircase and gallery, the dining room, drawing room and library. 'Unlike many estate houses, each room is very individual, with a very different feel,' explains Donal Woods, the production designer. 'The owners welcomed us with open arms and it was lovely to be back.' The treasures and furniture of the Carnarvons often stand in for those of the Crawleys. Portraits of Carnarvon family ancestors are left hanging during filming and Van Dyck's famous painting of Charles I still provides an impressive backdrop for dining room scenes.

As so many in the production crew were familiar with the house, the process of setting it up again for the film was fairly straightforward. Donal describes it as simply 'putting the odd photo up and adding furniture' although concessions are always made to protect the treasures of Highclere, with rubber sheets to protect its ancient floors and a white tablecloth on its antique dining table. The crew must also check for any modern items in and around the house, covering up everything from alarm sensors to radiators, and replacing the lanterns at the front of the house with ones suitable for the period.

Downton Abbey's location manager, Sparky Ellis, was also delighted to be back at Highclere, and liaised closely with Lord and Lady Carnarvon and their house manager John Gundill. 'It's a Grade I listed building, so you need to do things properly, and if you have eighty to ninety people suddenly descending on the house for the best part of two weeks, it can put an enormous strain on the property.'

Much of the joy of filming at Highclere is its grand exterior and grounds, and the production team were keen to capture the full splendour of the house and make the most of the beautiful landscape surrounding it for the big screen. To achieve this, director Michael Engler and director of photography Ben Smithard made use of drones, which have improved in reliability over the last two to three years, although the team needed to secure the relevant licence and approvals to fly them over Highclere. Once they did, however, they were able to capture some fantastic aerial footage.

Behind the Scenes
THE OPENING MONTAGE

The opening montage scene of the movie shows a crested letter making its way from Buckingham Palace, via King's Cross station in London, to Downton Abbey.

The production design team put in an immense amount of work into creating detailed authentic-looking props for *Downton Abbey*, including the letter from Buckingham Palace that we see winging its way to Yorkshire. Kimberley Bright, who handled many of the graphic props explains the process: 'Multiple copies of the letter were made for each stage of its journey and for

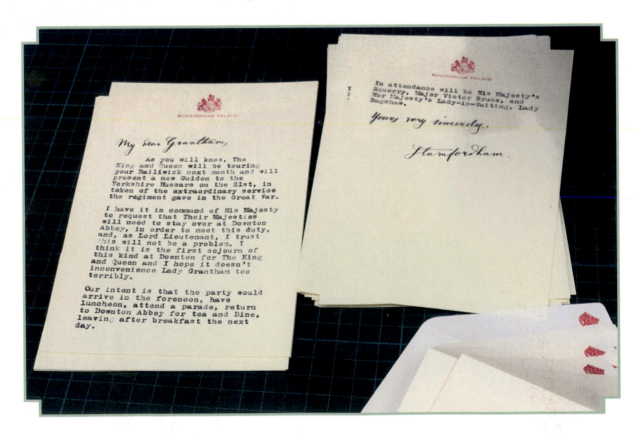

every take. We first see it signed by the King's Private Secretary, Stamfordham, so a new one was needed for each take of the signings. After its journey from Buckingham Palace via the postal train, Post Office and postman on his motorbike to Downton Abbey, we see the letter being opened and read by Lord Grantham. Again, this needed several copies so that he could open a fresh letter for each take.'

To recreate the letter paper, the Buckingham Palace crest was added by a letterpress company so it was slightly indented into the paper, as it would have been at the time. Historical advisor Alastair Bruce composed the wording of the letter, which was then typed on a 1920s typewriter: 'This added further texture and character as the age of the typewriter created slightly uneven and wonky text.'

Kimberley also made all the envelopes by hand and cut them to the much smaller size of letters in the period. As the King owned the Royal Mail, letters sent from Buckingham Palace didn't require postage stamps; their envelopes were franked with the 'Privy Purse' stamp.

The steam engine that we see thundering through the Yorkshire countryside – shot by the camera crew from a helicopter – is a Q6 no. 63395 locomotive. Built in 1918, it plied the tracks of north-east England for fifty years. Over 60 feet in length and weighing over 110 tons, it now belongs to the North Yorkshire Moors Railway Trust (NYMR). Its home at Pickering Station, also part of the NYMR, stood in for King's Cross. Pickering is a small rural station so the scene required a huge amount of post-production work by the visual effects team, replacing it with a much larger recreation of King's Cross based on photos from the era.

The train sorting room was filmed in a mail carriage supplied by the Great Central Railway Museum in Loughborough.

The footage of the letter on the final leg of its journey – a motorcyclist riding along the approach to Downton Abbey – was shot using a drone. As director of photography, Ben Smithard, explains: 'We wanted the opening scene to set the tone and give the film an epic quality right from the beginning.'

LORD and LADY GRANTHAM

Hugh Bonneville
Elizabeth McGovern

Downton Abbey is the home of the Earl and his wife the Countess of Grantham: Robert and Cora. No one is more aware of the weighty responsibilities they bear in protecting the estate where generations of Crawleys and their staff have lived and worked. As a boy, Robert ran along its corridors and its very bricks are part of him, his whole life dedicated to its care and safekeeping for future generations.

Over the years, Robert has had to face a changing world, and has wrestled with some tough decisions affecting his family, the estate and the household, the management of which is increasingly the realm of his eldest daughter, Mary. Nonetheless, while time has moved on to 1927, Downton Abbey still stands and life goes on for the Crawley family, as it has for generations. 'At the beginning of the movie, Lord Grantham is in a fairly calm place,' explains Hugh Bonneville, who plays the Earl. 'The world hasn't shifted on its axis and that's fine for a conservative like Robert.'

News of the royal visit, however, is set to puncture the quiet life that Lord Grantham cherishes, although he and the whole household are enormously proud to have King George V and Queen Mary visit their home. As a peer, Robert's loyalty is not only to his family and estate but also to the Crown, although this centuries-old allegiance must also be balanced against the pressures of the modern

world, which we see when Robert announces the impending royal visit just as Mary is worrying about paying for roof repairs.

In preparation for the arrival of the King and Queen, the house is thrown into a state of frenzied activity, 'It's like living in a factory,' remarks Robert as he walks past hordes of servants cleaning in the hallway. Meanwhile Cora enjoys the hustle and bustle of the pre-visit preparations, reminding her of life during the war when the house was turned into an officers' convalescence home.

In private, Robert and Cora admit they are excited by the visit, but outwardly they play the part of gracious hosts to perfection. Cora, originally an American heiress, has spent all her married life at Downton and she is well versed in the protocol required, executing an elegant curtsey when she first greets the royal couple.

Much of the turmoil, however, is below stairs, as Hugh explains: 'The Crawleys of course want to make it look like a royal visit is water off a duck's back, but – as with any water-and-duck scenario – there's a lot of paddling going on underneath. Downstairs the two

Robert: 'Are you excited?'

Cora: 'I am a bit. Are you?'

Robert: 'Is it common to admit it?'

Cora: 'Not to an American.'

tribes – the royal servants and the staff of Downton – are at war. While upstairs everything appears to be calm, all card games and tinkling glasses.'

Elizabeth McGovern, who plays Cora, revealed there was also something of a buzz on the set, the cast and crew conscious of the fact that they were working on a film. 'On the one hand, it was a bit like *Groundhog Day*, as many things hadn't changed and we slotted fairly quickly into the old rituals. But it was thrilling to work with actors I'd admired for many years and it was a real opportunity for the cinematographer to take it up a notch. And unbelievably my clothes were even more spectacular, the fabrics top of the line.'

Having played the role of Cora since the beginning of the show, Elizabeth found the royal element of the film's storyline interesting: 'The experience of being in the show is a bit like being in the royal

Cora: '. . . if I know anything about royal visits, we will never stop changing our clothes.'

family. Like the Queen, Cora is very visible and she is expected to play a part without necessarily doing a great deal and by doing so she seems to represent so much, the history and tradition.' The royal visit gives her a sense of purpose, while she also no doubt enjoys the glamour and drama of such a momentous occasion.

A loving wife and mother, Cora also proves herself an astute mediator within the family, which is no mean feat when it comes to relations with her indomitable mother-in-law Violet. In the movie, this skill is made evident when she manages to ensure the King withdraws his invitation for Bertie to escort the Prince of Wales on an overseas' tour – a gentle word in the Queen's ear is all that is needed to resolve the situation. Her motivation was Edith's evident distress when she discovered her husband would be going away when their baby was due.

Once the royal couple have left Downton, Cora and Robert are able to relax a little as they dance at the Harewood ball. Glowing in the success of the visit, Cora declares, 'I do love our adventures', to which Robert replies, 'But isn't it fun when they're over?' He's clearly happiest when life at Downton Abbey returns to a familiar rhythm.

'When we enter the story of the movie, time has moved on a little. Robert's grandchildren are a little bit older, but there haven't been drastic changes.'

Hugh Bonneville

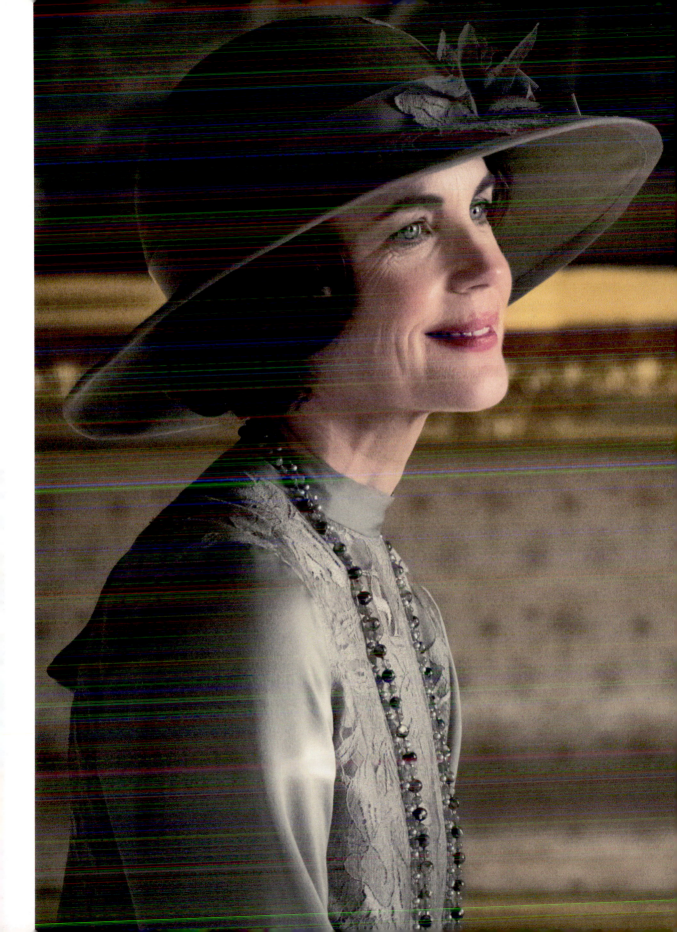

'Cora is wonderful to dress and I love the fact that she's American and very much a follower of fashion, but on a different level to her daughters. The design process for her outfits tends to be a little more organic and evolve gradually.'

Anna Robbins,
costume designer

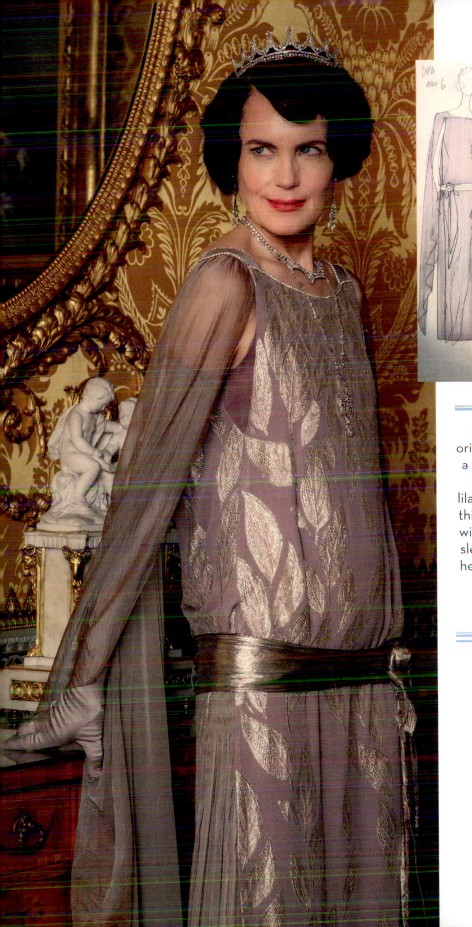

'For her ballgown we used original fabric, vintage lamé and a turquoise fabric with leaves, which we dyed a mauve-y lilac – a very Cora colour. Using this we created a draped dress with a cowled back and chiffon sleeves that cascades down to her ankles with a bit of a train.'

Anna Robbins,
costume designer

45

ANNA ROBBINS
Costume Designer

The costumes have always played a hugely important part in *Downton Abbey*, in recreating the period feel of the show, while also adding to the story of all its characters. For the movie, costume designer Anna Robbins oversaw the whole process, as she had done for the last two seasons of the television series. The standards that she and her team worked to on the show were already extremely high – as some of the dazzling on-screen creations testify – but for the movie they knew they had to raise their game even further.

Downton Abbey is also famed for its historical accuracy, so Anna was keen to ensure authenticity across all the classes. Her job initially was to move the characters into the late 1920s and to find that epitome of the decade's style. 'Fashion moves forward and never stands still, particularly women's fashion,' explains Anna, 'but it's still a rolling evolution, which in the TV series can be achieved by adding or changing little things. In a film, you obviously can't do that, and I had fewer costumes, so I really had to make my mark with each one.'

In preparing for any television series or film, Anna's first job is to get to know the characters really well and their place in the story. She also researches the period extensively, looking at books, historical references as well as images, both generally and those of real people depicted in the film. The Victoria and Albert Museum in London is an invaluable resource as she can view actual garments in their archives and see first-hand how they were constructed. Vintage clothes markets are also useful for research as well for sourcing actual garments for the show. Anna worked closely with John Bright at the costumier Cosprop, which specialises in the making and sourcing of authentic period costume for film, television and theatre.

'The men's clothes are largely tailored from scratch, mainly because the men in the 1920s tended to be much smaller with different body shapes, and tailoring new suits helped us to give them the right shape and proportion for the period.'

Anna has to consider carefully where each scene will be shot. She works with Donal Woods and the art department to look at fabrics and colours on the set, and also talks to Ben Smithard about the lighting. 'I look at each scene as a kind of composition, which needs to be painted beautifully, all of the costumes sitting really well together. It's all about looking at palette, texture and tone, and finding a combination for each character that symbolises what they represent.'

LADY MARY and HENRY TALBOT

Michelle Dockery
Matthew Goode

Over the years, we've watched Lady Mary grow from a girl to a woman; we've seen her incredible strength, tenacity and poise, a character who doesn't always do the right thing but who, ultimately, we can't help but admire. In the words of Michelle Dockery, who plays Mary: 'I've always loved her complexity. She's incredibly human – she can be as kind as she is mean. She goes to dark places, but is always learning.'

After a period of resistance, Mary finally succumbed to the charms of handsome racing car driver Henry Talbot and they are now happily married, with two children George, (her son from her first marriage to Matthew Crawley) and eighteen-month-old Caroline, who is a new addition to the family since we last met them.

Dashing Henry has charisma, says what he thinks and clearly adores Mary. They are both strong and stubborn, but entirely right for each other. Thankfully, Mary realised this at the end of the final season, putting aside her initial reservations over his 'adequate but not overwhelming prospects' and love of car racing. Now they are married, they are still blissfully in love, although Henry retains his independence by running a car showroom with Branson – when the film opens Henry is away at a motor show in Chicago – and is happy for Mary to take charge at Downton, where she has taken over much of the responsibility of running the estate.

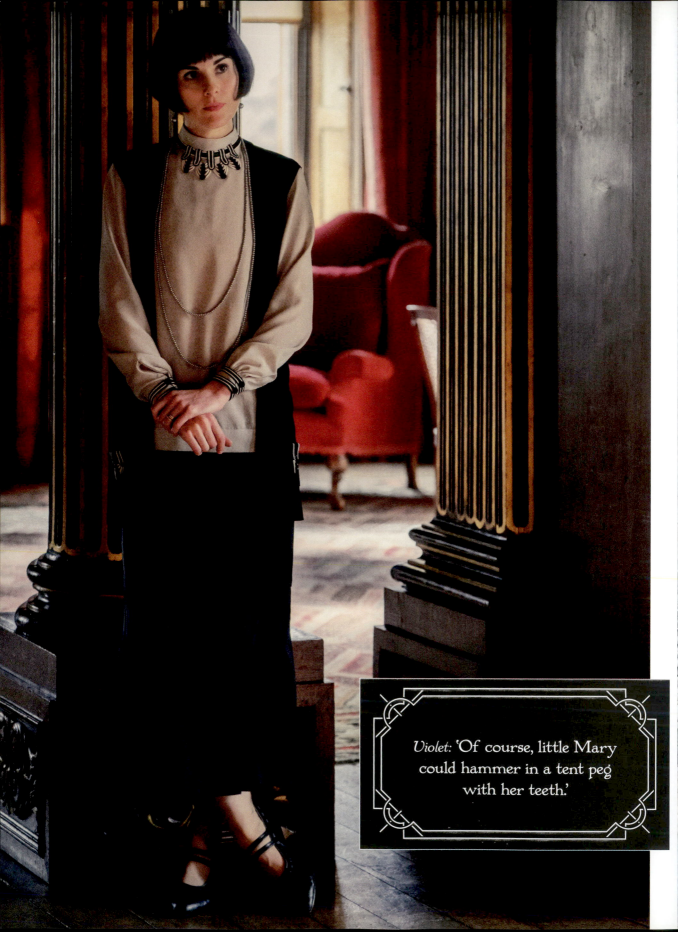

Violet: 'Of course, little Mary could hammer in a tent peg with her teeth.'

It is Mary now who frets over the weighty task of balancing the books and keeping everything going. As a result, when the royal visit is announced, Mary oversees preparations, both upstairs and down – a huge undertaking, as she constantly reminds everyone. She is, however, more than capable, soon commandeering the services of the recently retired Carson. Lord Grantham worries whether 'poor little Mary' has taken too much on. Violet is less doting and knows her granddaughter well: 'Of course, little Mary could hammer in a tent peg with her teeth.' And Mary is never afraid to roll up her sleeves either, as she helps to unload the chairs for the parade in pouring rain when they arrive unexpectedly during the buffet.

On coming back to the *Downton* set after a three-year hiatus, Michelle was thrilled to have the opportunity to return to Highclere and 'to be back with all the gang again'. While Michelle had seen some of the cast during the three years, she was reminded how much she'd enjoyed spending time with the people making the television series, such as her on-screen grandmother: 'Suddenly it all stops, so

'When we first started the series, we were all in corsets, with so many layers you could barely walk. To travel from that Edwardian style to the kind of thing we're wearing now has been amazing. In the first season I needed dressers to help me get in and out of costumes, whereas now I can just throw my costumes on in the morning.'

Michelle Dockery

of course we all missed each other. I saw Maggie [Smith] every day and then suddenly I wasn't seeing very much of her and I'd forgotten just how funny she is.'

Mary looks stunning in whatever she wears, but the 1920s styles suit her frame beautifully and Michelle has always been excited to see what she will be wearing on camera. 'On coming back to *Downton*, my first costume fitting was one of the most exciting of my whole career, because I just couldn't wait to see what they had in store. When Anna [Robbins] said she'd just been to Paris to find pieces for me, I was just chomping at the bit to see what she had brought back!'

In the privacy of her bedroom, Mary often talks frankly with her maid, Anna, and the two characters have developed a close relationship. Michelle was pleased to get back in front of the camera with Joanne Froggatt: 'I've always loved my scenes with Joanne so it was wonderful to play those again.' When the royal visit is almost over, it is to Anna that Mary confesses that she's pleased it went well but is not sure she could face it again.

Less harmonious is Mary's relationship with her sister, Edith, whose new-found happiness and status initially comes as something of a surprise to Mary, who had always belittled her little sister since nursery days. Edith has grown in confidence over the years, especially now she is happily married, and there is more of an equilibrium between the two siblings – although Mary still can't help but get in the odd dig at Edith as old habits die hard.

As self-assured as Mary seems, though, the responsibility of running the Downton estate weighs heavily on her mind, as she confides to Anna and her grandmother Violet. It is clearly a struggle and she worries whether keeping Downton going is worth it, 'when the world it was built for is fading with every day that passes'. Anna reminds her what Downton Abbey means to the people who live and work there, how it is the heart of the community not just for them but for the village and county too. Violet similarly dismisses Mary's concerns, impressing on her that Mary is the future of Downton Abbey – that she will take over from Violet as the 'frightening old lady who keeps everyone up to the mark'.

Mary: 'Never mind. You're here now. And I don't have to go to the ball alone like a sad little wallflower.'

Henry: 'I'll only come if you promise to dance with me, non-stop.'

Mary: 'Oh, it's a deal.'

Of Mary and Henry's future together, Matthew Goode, who plays Henry, says, 'He's quite a modern character and I think in ten or fifteen years, he will have relaxed the code a little bit at Downton. I doubt you'll see him in white tie and stockings again. And of course he drives, and you don't get much more modern than that – he embraces technology and I think we can all relate to the thrill you get putting your foot down in one of those cars.' Ultimately, of course, he's happy to be with Mary, to dance all night with her at the ball and to remain at Downton – 'Leave Downton? I think we're stuck with it, aren't we?' he says to Mary as they dance.

With Henry at her side, the future does indeed look rosy, and Mary knows in her heart that she will battle on for the sake of the family, for Violet and the future descendants of the Crawleys. If anyone can keep Downton Abbey going it's Mary, and we can't help but feel it's in safe hands.

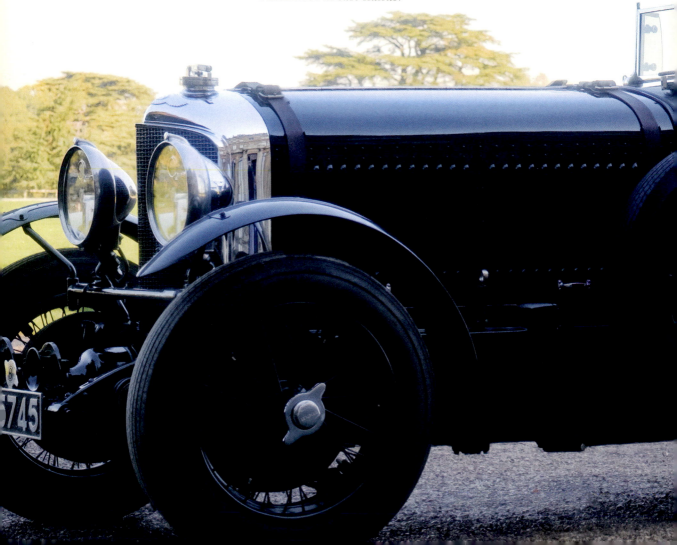

In 1927, waistlines had dropped right down to the hip – it was all about long lines and free movement; corsets had gone, a reflection of the emancipation of women. Clothing was softer and more comfortable – women were more active so their clothing needed to be practical.

'Edith and Mary are both career women. Mary is managing the estate and is very much a woman in a man's world. She wears a lot of ties and waistcoats and she looks wonderful in androgynous tailoring, which is fabulous for that era.'

Anna Robbins,
costume designer

For the dinner at Downton Abbey with the King and Queen, costume designer Anna Robbins dressed Mary in a reimagined Delphos gown.

The original Fortuny gowns were created in the style of an ancient Greek tunic, the chiton. First available around 1907, the dress attracted immediate recognition, its free-flowing shape a world away from the tightly corseted fashions of previous years. Originally worn as more of an informal gown by avant-garde actresses such as Sarah Bernhardt, the dress was later taken up by well-to-do women like Mary as acceptable evening wear.

Anna first worked with the legendary textile house Fortuny on the final series of Downton Abbey and her ongoing relationship with them led to collaboration with the heritage textile company to create this bespoke pleated gown for Mary for the film. This unique dress is neither vintage nor a copy, it is a 'brand new' original created using the famous and secret pleating technique developed by Mariano Fortuny and his wife and muse, Henriette.

'It has taken Fortuny years of development to unlock the secrets of the pleat and I knew that with this reclaimed technique I had a unique opportunity to work with them on this gown for Mary. The silk was dyed to a brilliant, rich Prussian blue that becomes more luminous after pleating. The gown is entirely hand sewn and the pleated silk skims the body and pools effortlessly on to the floor.'

Anna Robbins,
costume designer

59

'Where I could, I would use original pieces. Beaded dresses tend to be original because to bead a dress to couture level could cost tens or even thousands of pounds to make, which the *Downton* budget wouldn't quite stretch to! I might build in an original beaded panel or piece of fabric into a dress. We had an amazing workroom and a beader who helped customise original dresses, such as Mary's ballgown which is half 1920s and half 2018!'

Anna Robbins,
costume designer

Country Estates

The estate over which Mary presides would have been much larger than the house and the servants that work in it. Stretching across several thousand acres, it includes a home farm, which supplies the house with food and produce, tenant farms, cottages, woods, shooting ranges, lakes, gardens and a park. Workers on the estate – from gardeners, farmers and carpenters – would vastly outnumber servants in the house and would have been recruited from the local village, with other workers living in estate cottages.

When it comes to the survival of the Downton estate, Mary is capable of making tough decisions, which is just as well as great landowners across the country were struggling to make ends meet. For estates like Downton Abbey, farming was central to their existence. Landowners had to innovate to find ways to survive at a time when the countryside was sinking into depression as prices of farming products dropped and rural populations dwindled.

Since the end of the First World War, country estates had laboured under a much heavier burden of taxation, and many of their owners were forced to sell part if not all of their estates. While land was increasingly subject to heavy income tax, money earned from its sale could be kept tax free, which encouraged estate owners to sell parts of their property, often to tenant farmers. Death duties had risen again in 1919 and servants' wages had also experienced a sharp rise.

It is against this backdrop – with many great estates being sold, broken up and even demolished – that Mary is striving to hold on to Downton Abbey, a not-inconsiderable task.

ANNE 'NOSH' OLDHAM

Hair and Make-up Designer

Having worked on the first two seasons of *Downton Abbey*, Anne Oldham, known as Nosh, was delighted and flattered to be invited back by the production team to work on the film. Although she was familiar with the series and the team behind it, she was keen to refresh the look of the characters while keeping everything very much within the *Downton* mould. 'Our goal was to heighten and polish, and to bring everything forward a couple of years,' explains Nosh.

Now that *Downton* was to appear on the big screen, Nosh needed to push even further that attention to detail, checking and re-checking everything before the camera rolled. 'We also had a really good camera team, headed up by Ben Smithard. He and I talked about the lighting for the scenes, as this hugely affects how people look on screen. Our goal was that in the daytime our female characters wouldn't look too made-up – they should appear polished but in a natural way, especially for the characters downstairs. In the evenings, women can wear visible make-up but again we were careful here – lipsticks and eyebrows were a little stronger at that time and we might do a little nod to that but we wanted

the upstairs ladies to look glamorous but not make them look like flapper girls as that would have been a little extreme.'

When *Downton Abbey* first came on our television screens, Nosh and the rest of the team worked hard to establish the eighteen main characters, each with their own silhouette and look, so that even if you only saw the back of their heads you would know instinctively who they were. This means that although characters' hairstyles may have evolved over the years, no one's appearance is radically changed.

For the film, all the new characters needed to be similarly distinguishable from the rest of the cast. Nosh felt that she needed to spend as much time and effort as possible on the new cast members, giving them the same attention to detail as everyone else.

Before any filming happens, Nosh does full hair and make-up tests with the actors, fitting wigs that have been made, and then making any revisions that are required. 'You want the actors to feel completely at home in their look,' explains Nosh, 'so they're feeling confident and ready for that first day of filming.'

LORD and LADY HEXHAM

Harry Hadden-Paton
Laura Carmichael

Edith is now happily married to 'one of the grandest men in England' (as her father once described him), her very own prince charming Bertie Pelham. Living at his family seat of Brancaster Castle with Edith's daughter, Marigold, the couple have the rather grand titles of Marquess and Marchioness of Hexham.

Bertie unexpectedly inherited his title – one that outranks an earl – just before he and Edith married but their subsequent rise in social status hasn't gone to their heads. They are still very much the forward-thinking couple they were before their marriage, shocking Edith's parents when they turn up at Downton without so much as a nanny or a valet. 'It's 1927,' announces Bertie. 'We're modern folk.'

Edith's modern outlook on life is mirrored in her fashionable appearance, and after arriving at Downton she's keen to see the new ballgown she has ordered from the atelier of well-known fashion designer Madame Handley-Seymour. Laura Carmichael, who plays Edith, was similarly keen to see some of the wardrobe department's creations for the film, which included an original beaded dress as well as tiaras, which Edith can wear now she's married. 'The costumes are stunning, as are the locations,' enthused Laura. '*Downton* has always looked beautiful but everything has gone up a notch for the movie and to see that energy making it all perfect has been very exciting.'

'Edith went from having long hair to a shorter cut with a wave; now life has really changed for her we needed to show that she'd moved on, while still being very much the Edith we know.'

**Nosh Oldham,
hair and make-up designer**

Edith's ballgown is late to arrive and then a similar dress turns up in the wrong size. While Edith appears to fret about the dress, she does have more serious issues to consider, namely that she thinks she is pregnant, as she later confesses to Bertie. Naturally, they are both delighted, although the news is marred by the fact that the King has asked Bertie to join his son, the Prince of Wales, on a long foreign tour at the time the baby is due. Bertie is torn between duty to his King and his obvious longing to be close by as Edith brings his first child into the world. Fortunately for Edith and Bertie, Cora and

Edith: 'I just want to own my own life. I want to say things that I think, and do what I like.'

Queen Mary manage to advise the King that now is not the time for the Marquess to head off overseas.

'The idea that Bertie might be away when she is due to have the baby,' explains Laura, 'stirs up these feelings with Edith, about the lack of control she has and she misses her old life working in London as a magazine editor.' Having already had a taste of independence, Edith's new-found position as a marchioness 'entertaining people who bore me to death' is trying – as she says, 'I just want to own my own life. I want to say things that I think, and do what I like.'

Luckily for Edith, she has a husband who is more than willing to support her. 'They are ahead of the time,' explains Harry Hadden-Paton, who plays Bertie, 'and I think Bertie is in awe of Edith and her strength and he wants to facilitate that. He's a sensitive character and does the right thing.'

While Bertie is certainly considerate, there is also a gung-ho side to him. The evening before the parade, just as everyone is helping themselves to a buffet dinner, he heads off into a stormy night in search of Branson, who has mysteriously disappeared. 'I like to think he had a good war and is happy to get stuck in if he's needed,' says Harry.

However, not all aspects of filming were plain-sailing for Harry, as he explains: 'Edith and Bertie arrive at Downton in this wonderful 1920s car. The only issue was I was shown the car about ten minutes before I was due to drive it up to the house. The brakes are very different from modern cars, meaning I had to start applying the brakes about a hundred metres before I would normally and then make sure the car stopped at a particular line for the shot. I then had to put the handbrake on, turn the engine off and try and open this really old-fashioned door, all the while looking like I knew exactly what I was doing.'

In playing Bertie, Harry delighted in his character's new-found membership of the Downton family. 'Having been a bit of an

outsider, Bertie is now very much part of their world and even helps to welcome in the new guests at Downton' – as Harry himself did on set with the arrival of the new members of the cast.

With a new baby on the way, life for the Hexhams is looking very bright. Edith has certainly had her share of heartache over the years and growing up under the shadow of her beautiful sisters once did little for her self-esteem. But she seems to shaken off all of that, and while her relationship with Mary will never be harmonious, even her sister can see Edith has become someone who is at last happy and sure of what she wants in life.

'I thought I might feel nervous coming back on set and filming for the big screen but actually it felt like returning to a character and family I know and love. In many ways, it's like we never left – like we're just back at our big house.'

Laura Carmichael

For ladies like Edith, the etiquette surrounding gloves was intricate. They could be removed during the day but evening gloves had to be kept on, other than while eating when a lady must place them on her lap – although it was acceptable to drink a glass of champagne in gloves.

'In 1927 where we are in the film, hemlines had almost reached their shortest point so you'd nearly see women's knees. Towards the end of the decade, the hem would drop back down again, with longer dresses all the rage again in the 1930s. It was great to show a bit of leg in the film!'

Anna Robbins,
costume designer

◄ Lady Astor entering Parliament in 1920.

▼ Actress Colleen Moore in 1929; she played the first 'bright young thing' on film in 1923.

Women in the 1920s

By 1927, women like Edith and Mary were able to lead quite different lives to those of their mothers or grandmothers. Edith has had a career, running a magazine in London, and yearns to return to the independence she once had. Mary is now largely running Downton Abbey and its estate, and is happy to muck in wherever she's needed.

Of course, there have always been robust, intelligent women at Downton Abbey, but it's hard to imagine Violet hopping over a stile to help out at the estate's pig farm, as Mary did in season four (although she'd probably have quite firm views on how it should be run).

Edith and Mary's new-found liberties are representative of the freedoms a whole generation of women were experiencing in the 1920s, particularly those with money and power. In 1918, women over the age of thirty had been given the vote and by 1928 this would be extended to all women over the age of twenty-one. By 1927, there had been seven female MPs; the first of these was Lady Astor, who continued working in the House of Commons until 1945.

As a result, women felt more confident and empowered, their independence reflected in new fashions – hair was shorter, hemlines were higher, corsets abandoned. It became acceptable for women to smoke, to drive motor cars and to have leisure interests, like the cinema. Some upper- and middle-class women took to frequenting cocktail bars and jazz bars, their decadent behaviour prompting the tabloid press to nickname their set the 'bright young things'.

TOM BRANSON

Allen Leech

Tom Branson is now settled at Downton Abbey, living there with his daughter, Sybbie, while running a car showroom with Henry and helping Mary to manage the estate. He is, if nothing else, busy. But he still hasn't found the happiness in love he once had with Sybil, the youngest of the Crawley daughters, who tragically died giving birth to Sybbie seven years earlier.

Branson entered the world of Downton Abbey as the family chauffeur, an Irishman who fervently believed in the independence of Ireland, in socialism and the abolition of monarchy. After losing his wife, he left with Sybbie for America, only to return to Downton Abbey so that his daughter could grow up with her family. Over the years he has sometimes struggled to adjust to living with the Crawleys – as he confesses to Maud Bagshaw's maid, Lucy, in the movie: 'Between my old world and new one, there were times when I didn't know who I was.' It's a journey we've watched Branson go on, as Allen Leech, who plays Tom, explains: 'Branson's always been slightly baffled by the aristocracy and their ways, and probably sees them in a similar way to the audience of *Downton*.'

Slowly but surely, however, Branson began to see the good side of the Crawleys, and the shared commitment in the management of the estate gave him a valued role. Once a strident revolutionary, he has gradually mellowed – 'I'm a law-and-order man these days.' Accepting that there are plenty of things he and the Crawleys disagree on – 'I wouldn't give tuppence for their politics' – he's nonetheless learned to be happy at Downton.

Branson: 'Between my old world and the new one, there were times when I didn't know who I was.'

In the series, Branson's look often echoed his Irish roots; he'd be dressed in Irish Donegal tweeds or similar materials. For the film, the wardrobe department marked his full transition to the upper class and there's no longer any difference in the way he and the Crawley men dress. 'For that reason, I echoed Robert's tweed choices in Branson's suits,' explains Anna Robbins, 'although we cut and styled them slightly differently to suit his character and age.'

While the family have accepted him into the fold, certain members begin to question whether the royal visit is sparking republican tendencies in Branson – although Mary, who has grown close to her brother-in-law, outwardly dismisses the notion, declaring he would never harm the family. Nevertheless, she is relieved to be proved right. When Branson first meets the strange establishment figure of Major Chetwode at his car showroom in York, he believes Chetwode is some

sort of government agent keeping him under surveillance during the royal visit. When Chetwode then asks Branson some odd questions over drinks at the King's Arms pub in the village, Branson suspects that it is in fact Chetwode who is a danger to the King, although he keeps his thoughts to himself.

Branson's suspicions, however, are confirmed at the royal parade the next day. Tom follows Chetwode as the parade passes through the village and heroically manages to wrestle him to the ground just before he tries to shoot the King on horseback. 'That makes a good turn in the film,' says Allen. 'Everyone had him wrong. Tom was actually looking after the family, and because of that looked after the royal family at the same time.'

Having saved the life of the King at the parade, Branson also unwittingly helps the King's daughter, Princess Mary, when they talk in the grounds of the house. He is entirely unaware of her status – and would probably be less in awe of her than others might be if he did know – and she is touched and interested to hear about the compromises he's made in living at Downton.

'Allen Leech is a good friend and like my brother, so much so that sometimes he'll come up and pinch my arm just to annoy me. But it is such fun working with your mates – it's just the best job in the world.'

Michelle Dockery

'We were a family for six years and you go away, do your own thing for three years, and you come back and you almost pick up conversations that you left off exactly three years ago. It's great.'

Allen Leech

Branson also impresses another person connected with the royals, namely Lucy Smith, the maid of Lady Bagshaw. There is an instant spark of romance between the two – strengthened by the fact that they have both entered the aristocratic world by irregular means – she as the secret illegitimate daughter of Lady Bagshaw and Branson as a chauffeur. As Allen says, 'Lucy is someone whose life is about to be turned upside down in a similar way that Branson's was. He immediately feels an attraction to her, but also an affiliation with her situation. The irony is, however, that if he were ever to marry Lucy, these two outsiders would inherit the estate of Lady Bagshaw; which under normal circumstances would have passed to Lord Grantham – not that Branson is motivated by any of this.

Just as the Crawley family have warmed to Branson, so have we the viewers – he deserves love again and we hope that he's finally found it. As Allen says, 'It's what I think the fans would want and we wanted to make sure that Branson had an opportunity to find happiness again.'

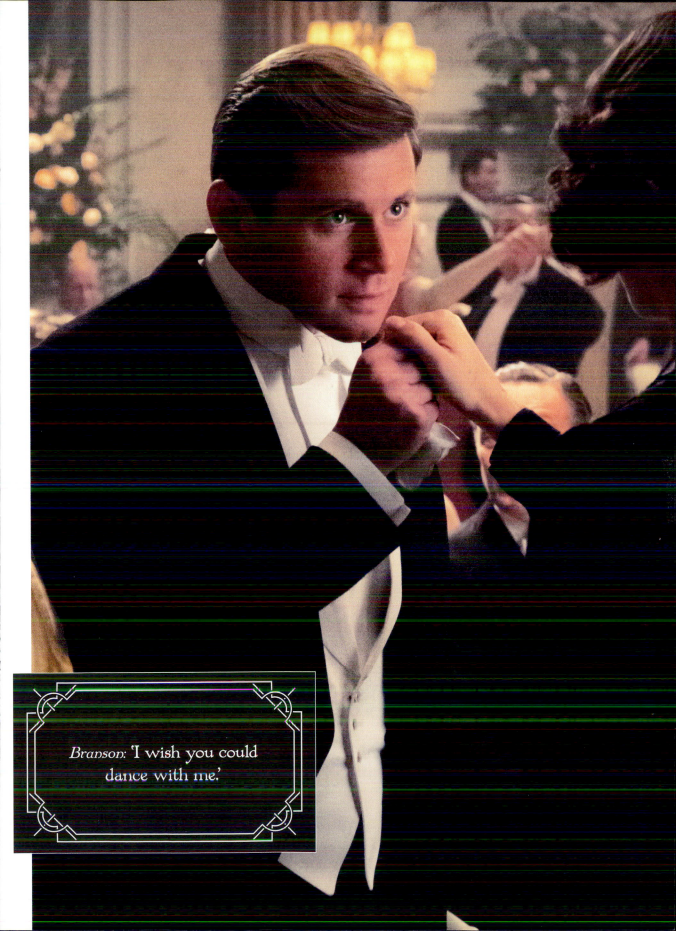

Branson: 'I wish you could dance with me.'

The attire for men at the dinner with the royal couple at Downton and the ball at Harewood is 'court dress', which means 'white tie' from the waist up, with black breeches, knee-length silk stockings and court shoes below. To recreate the look, the wardrobe department referred to paintings and photographs of George V. They also used various books on etiquette and dress from the time and liaised with the historical advisor, Alastair Bruce.

'It is a bit of a challenge getting back into the white tie and tails, with collars that are like razor blades. I can't imagine how they managed to have relaxed evenings when they had what feels like a piece of steel down the front of their chest.'

Hugh Bonneville

VIOLET, DOWAGER COUNTESS of GRANTHAM

Maggie Smith

The family matriarch, Violet, the Dowager Countess, has always fiercely protected the Crawley family and its estate. She is a firm believer in the rules of social hierarchy and as such her allegiance to the King and Queen is unshakeable. More problematic is her opinion of the Queen's lady-in-waiting Lady Bagshaw, whom we discover is a relation of the Crawleys but who has mysteriously cut herself off from the family.

It emerges that Lord Grantham is in fact the rightful heir to Maud Bagshaw's estate, although Violet suspects she is to write Robert out of her will. Incensed by the very thought of this, the former mistress of Downton Abbey is set to fight tooth and claw for what she believes is rightfully her son's. Her eventual showdown with Maud proves predictably feisty, particularly when Violet discovers that Maud's maid is her chosen heir. Violet rages – '…you are clearly insane! You should be in an asylum!'

Fortunately for everyone, Isobel steps in, having worked out for herself Lady Bagshaw's secret – that Lucy is in fact Maud's illegitimate daughter – and advises Maud to tell Violet. When Violet is enlightened, she doesn't approve but she understands the situation and instead resolves to encourage the blossoming union between Tom and Lucy, having not quite given up the fight to get Brompton Park back 'for Tom at least'.

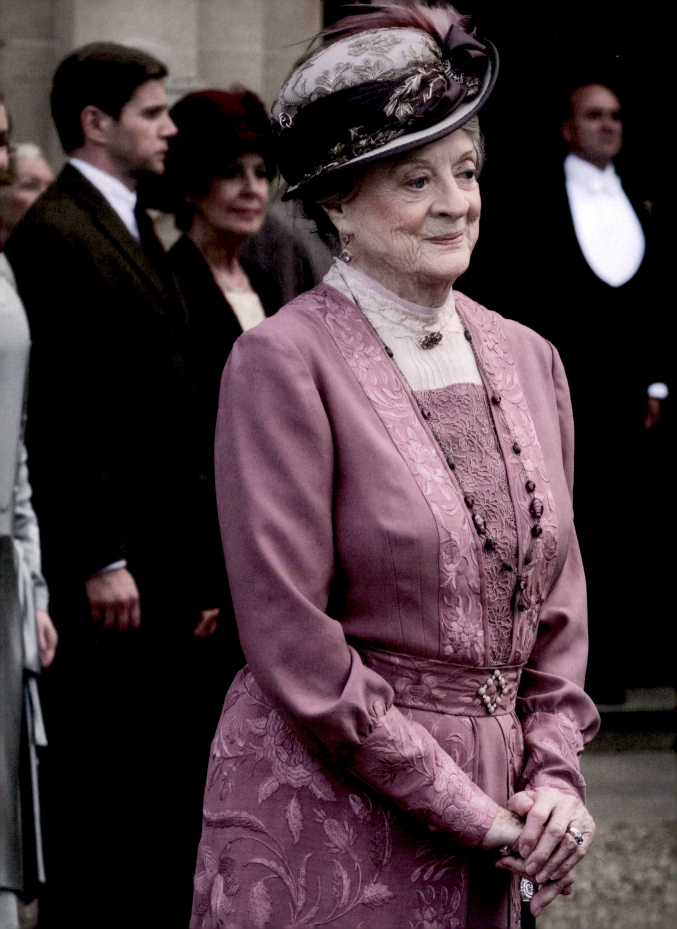

The whole affair illustrates just how formidable a foe Violet can be, although she is not as shocked by Lady Bagshaw's predicament as one might expect, hinting that she is a little more worldly than others give her credit for. Born in 1842, Violet would have had a strait-laced Victorian upbringing, but over the years she has had to adjust to changes and potential scandal within her own family – her granddaughter Sybil married Branson when he was just the family chauffeur, while Edith went on to have an illegitimate daughter, Marigold. Violet ultimately embraces both within the

Violet: 'To treat your maid as a blood relation is to unpick every fibre of the English way of life.'

family (although she still hasn't quite got over the passing of white tie and tiaras at dinner). In the final season, we also discovered that Violet once had a brief love affair with a Russian prince, a tantalising glimpse of her younger days.

Beneath her haughty demeanour, Violet does have a softer side and will go to great lengths to ensure the happiness of those she holds dear. Despite her initial misgivings about Isobel, who has a far more liberal view of the world than the Dowager Countess, Violet has grown fond of the plain-speaking Lady Merton and has proved a staunch support for her friend, although the two still seem to delight in their verbal spats. Isobel works hard to get Violet and Lady Bagshaw together so they can discuss their dispute over the Brompton estate, which Violet acknowledges, although she sees it as more of an opportunity to have Lady Bagshaw 'cornered'.

Violet's sharp tongue and her witty one-liners are defining characteristics of the Dowager Countess – never more so than in the film, which includes a wealth of such examples. Julian Fellowes of course writes the wonderful lines that Maggie Smith, who has won a Golden Globe for her portrayal of Violet, delivers so perfectly – it's a combination that makes for exquisite drama. As Julian himself has said, he asks a lot of Maggie as an actress, as she is required to make the viewers laugh and cry, sometimes in the same scene, which she does to remarkable effect in her touching scene with Mary at the ball.

Above all else, Violet is committed to her family, and entrusts the future of Downton Abbey to her granddaughter Mary. In the film's most poignant scene, she confesses to Mary that she does not have long to live and that it is Mary who must take over when she is gone: 'You are the best of me that will live on'. On the brink of the grave, as she puts it, Violet allows herself a little sentimentality with Mary, but refuses to wallow in self-pity – she has never been one to burden anyone with her own grief. 'The point is, I'll be fine until I'm not. That's all there is to it,' she says as she and Mary leave to join the ball – the past and future chatelaines of Downton Abbey.

Mary: 'You know you'll always be with us, Granny, staring from every picture, talking from every book, as long as the house stands.'

Violet: ' Sounds very exhausting. Do you know, I think I should prefer to rest in peace.'

Isobel: 'And you're an expert
in the matter?'

Violet: 'Oh, I'm an expert in
every matter.'

Behind the Scenes

THE GRAND DINNER

King George: 'This is good. I thought something else was planned, but it is excellent, so "well done" to old Courbet.'

Molesley: 'Oh, this wasn't Monsieur Courbet, Your Majesty. Mrs Patmore cooked it. In fact, it is the Downton Abbey staff who are serving you this evening.'

A key scene in the film is the evening dinner, where the King and Queen are obviously the very special guests of honour. With the table dressed beautifully and guests in their finery, dining room scenes make for a wonderful spectacle in *Downton Abbey*. The grandeur and formality of evening dinners also provide plenty of scope for dramatic tension, which is multiplied by at least ten when the King and Queen are at the table.

At Downton Abbey, evening dinners are still very much formal events – the footmen serve from the left, supervised by the butler who is stationed close to the sideboard, from which he dispenses wine or other alcoholic drinks. Most evenings, the women wear formal evening dress and the men now wear black tie. They once wore white tie and tailcoats, but by 1927 this is only brought out, along with tiaras for the ladies, for very special occasions – and there is no occasion more special than having the King and Queen to dinner. Nevertheless, dining at Downton is a little more relaxed than the royal family's own formal

dinners, where King George V and Queen Mary observed strict protocol. At Windsor Castle, the Guards string band played 'God Save the King' behind a grille as guests assembled for dinner, the meal lasted no longer than an hour, the post-meal coffee and port just twenty minutes, with the King and Queen retiring at eleven o'clock on the dot. 'Nothing was lacking but gaity,' recalled their son, the future Edward VIII.

Set decorator Gina Cromwell and her team dressed the table with an exquisite flower display in regal colours running down the centre, featuring red roses and orchids. The finest glasses, china and silverware are also on the table, along with menu cards. Historical advisor Alastair Bruce and a former Buckingham Palace butler ensured everything was done correctly.

At the table, the Queen is seated to the left of Lord Grantham, in the middle, and the King is on the opposite side of the table, on Lady Grantham's left. The remaining fourteen guests are seated so that women and men alternate, with husbands and

wives apart. Food is served and cleared from the left, starting with the King and Queen, and drinks come in from the right. During a meal, guests would speak to their neighbour on one side for the first course, and on the other side for the second, after which the rules would be more relaxed. Ladies at the table had to observe which way the most senior woman – in this case Queen Mary – turned first and follow suit: in the film, Violet berates her granddaughter for talking in the wrong direction.

With eighteen people sitting at the table and the production crew encircling it, the dining room itself can get very busy. For the camera and lighting team, night shoots are particularly tricky. The silver candelabras are a focal point of the table decorations, and would have been the only light

At the Downton Abbey dinner, Queen Mary wears a reproduction of a diamond tiara that may be familiar to some viewers – it is worn by Queen Elizabeth on British banknotes. Named after the committee of women who raised money for its creation, the Girls of Great Britain and Ireland Tiara was given to Queen Mary (then Duchess of York) in 1893. She in turn gave it to her granddaughter Princess Elizabeth as a wedding present in 1947 and she has worn it regularly throughout her reign, still referring to it as 'Granny's Tiara'.

source. To create the necessary flickering effect and light the room effectively, director of photography Ben Smithard and his team floated a large balloon contraption above the table. 'It's illuminated from the inside,' explains Ben, 'and it floats because it's full of helium. By dimming the lights right down you get close to the feel of candlelight. With two to three cameras moving around the table, we were really tight on room, and this was the most space-effective way of lighting the scene.'

The filming of dining-room scenes at Highclere is a challenge for the cast as well as the crew. The actors must remain seated at the table for long periods of time while the camera and lighting team set up for multiple takes. The scene needs to be filmed from several angles, each line repeated many times, while cameras are rearranged, lighting adjusted and lavish piles of food are brought in and out many times.

However, it's probably most tiring for the actors playing the serving staff as they must remain on their feet whenever the cameras are rolling during the ten-hour filming day, usually with next to no dialogue. It's an occupational hazard for actors like Jim Carter, who as Carson has spent many stationary hours by the sideboard. He jokes that over the years he's developed a zen-like patience during the whole process. 'In the dining room, I'm more of a reactive presence, standing in the background raising eyebrows now and then disapprovingly. Of course, you never know what will get picked up in the final edit – sometimes you think you've been doing some amazing stuff only to be replaced with a close-up of some knives and forks. I'm pretty philosophical about all of that.'

Continuity is also a real challenge: for each take, the production team must ensure that the amount of food on the plates, the levels of wine in the glasses and even the heights of the burning candles are exactly the same. The servants must serve the food at precisely the right line in the script, without dropping anything and without clattering the serving utensils too much.

'Filming all the dinner scenes takes an age,' explains Douglas Reith, who plays Lord Merton. 'If you have anything to say, you end up saying it about thirty-eight times! And each time you shoot, you have to think about exactly what you were doing, were you drinking from a wine glass or holding a fork.'

It's all a tightly choreographed process, which makes for very long days of filming, and while the original *Downton Abbey* cast are well used to this, it was a first for Simon Jones, who plays King George. However, he soon learned how the actors at the table kill time as they wait between takes: 'Hugh [Lord Grantham] would pass round two salt cellars, each containing pieces of paper,' explains Simon. 'Whoever received the paper with the cross on it was the "murderer" and they had to surreptitiously wink at someone else at the table. They'd then wait a few seconds and die spectacularly. Allen [Tom Branson] was superb as a murderer, I think he managed to do away with everyone at the table.'

For a dinner party scene, careful planning goes into the menu, as Lisa Heathcote, home economist for *Downton*, explains: 'Dining room scenes involve long days of filming and the food has to be removed and refreshed as we go along.' There are many takes, meaning that each time an actor cuts into a particular food it then has to be replaced for a retake.

As a result, Lisa must cook in bulk and supply multiple batches of each food to ensure continuity. 'I also have to bear in mind how the food is served, that the actors will need to take food from a dish served by a footman so I need to prepare individual portions that can be easily handled. If I did one big jelly and then each actor takes a spoon out of it, I'd have to make hundreds of the same jelly, which logistically wouldn't work.

The actors also have to nibble on food throughout the day so I often put watercress and cucumber on the plates, because that's something you can eat lots of without feeling too nauseous at the end of the day!'

LORD and LADY MERTON

Douglas Reith
Penelope Wilton

Isobel and Lord Merton are now, much to the relief of everyone at Downton Abbey, a married couple. It took some time for Lord Merton to woo Isobel Crawley – particularly as they thought at one point that Lord Merton was to die from anaemia (but fortunately it turned out not to be the pernicious kind). Now living at Isobel's home, Crawley House, in the village, they are very much part of the family at Downton.

Brought up as a peer, Lord Merton is from a distinctly aristocratic background, very different to his more middle-class wife. Isobel's upbringing was more modest than those at Downton; her father and first husband were both doctors and she is a trained nurse. She came to Downton when her son, Matthew Crawley, unexpectedly became heir to the estate. Matthew was to fall in love with and marry Lady Mary, securing the future of Downton for the Crawleys. When he died tragically in a car crash, his mother, perhaps surprisingly, decided to stay on. 'The sense of privilege they all have at Downton grates with her a bit,' explains Penelope Wilton, who plays Isobel. 'She has come from a completely different background to the one she finds herself in and brings a sort of everyman's view to it all. She's not backward in coming forward with her criticism, although she's tremendously grateful for the Crawley family's warmth and how they looked after her when her son died.'

Isobel discovers that despite Lord Merton's upbringing, he is forward-thinking and cares little for snobbery or status, giving away his estate to his son, with whom he has fallen out. 'He doesn't wear his coronet on his sleeve,' says Douglas Reith, who plays him. As a result, the couple have an easy-going relationship and Lord Merton tends to laugh off Isobel's sniffy references about the King and Queen, a gentle foil to Isobel's uneasiness about the trappings of class, and rather more accepting of the opulence surrounding the royal party.

The two actors were delighted to be back with old friends on the *Downton Abbey* set, not least because it meant returning to Highclere, as Douglas explains: 'The wonderful thing about Highclere is that it's a private house, and quite intimate when you're inside. As soon as you walk through the doors, you feel welcomed.' All of Isobel and Lord Merton's scenes in the film are above stairs in the movie: they are guests at the afternoon tea with the royal couple, the lavish dinner in the evening and attend the ball at Harewood.

Violet: 'Will you have enough clichés to get you through the visit?'

Isobel: 'If not, I'll come to you.'

As a voice of dissent at Downton, Isobel was always destined to clash with the uncompromising Violet. Nonetheless, over the years their relationship has evolved into one of friendship, as Penelope describes: 'At the beginning they were absolute opposites and didn't like each other at all, but they've grown to admire and respect one another. Although they can't help teasing each other, which they still do a great deal.'

In the movie, Isobel, who is resourceful and ever-practical, attempts to get to the truth behind the relationship of Maud and her maid, Lucy, and by doing so deftly smooths over the long-standing feud between Violet and Lady Bagshaw. Despite their differences, Isobel has grown fond of Violet and is familiar with the peculiar workings of her mind – the two are a formidable match for each other.

'Isobel's dresses have a dropped waist but her hemlines were never above mid-calf and she wore relatively sensible shoes with a modest neckline and sleeve length.'

Anna Robbins, costume designer

A VILLAGE FIT FOR A KING

The village of Downton has always been of great importance to the Crawley family and the estate workers. For the film, two locations stood in for the village: Bampton in Oxfordshire, which was previously used for the television series, and Lacock in Wiltshire, which stood in for the splendid street scenes of the King's parade.

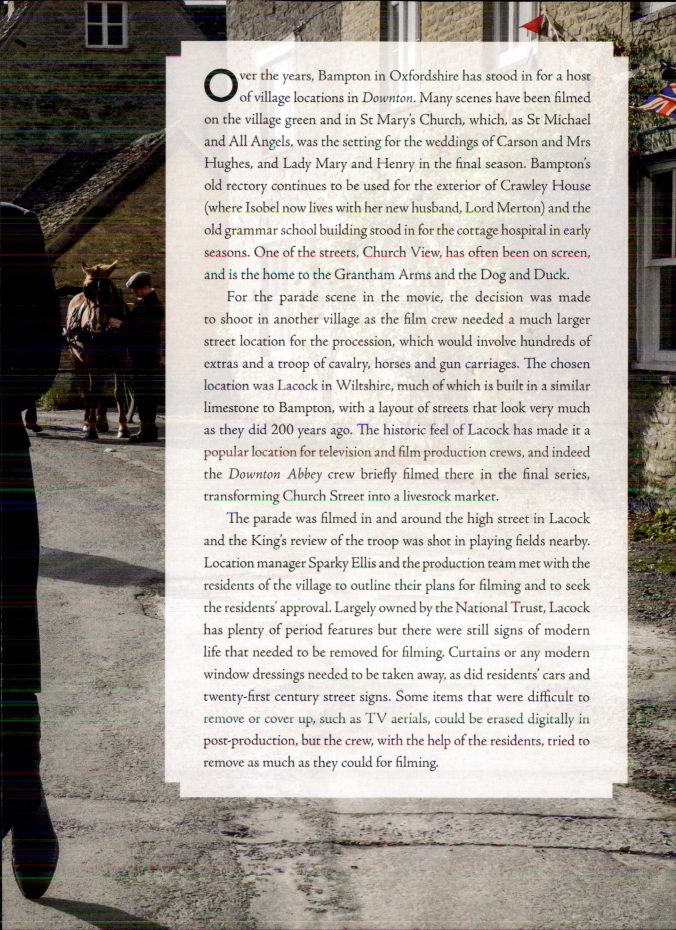

Over the years, Bampton in Oxfordshire has stood in for a host of village locations in *Downton*. Many scenes have been filmed on the village green and in St Mary's Church, which, as St Michael and All Angels, was the setting for the weddings of Carson and Mrs Hughes, and Lady Mary and Henry in the final season. Bampton's old rectory continues to be used for the exterior of Crawley House (where Isobel now lives with her new husband, Lord Merton) and the old grammar school building stood in for the cottage hospital in early seasons. One of the streets, Church View, has often been on screen, and is the home to the Grantham Arms and the Dog and Duck.

For the parade scene in the movie, the decision was made to shoot in another village as the film crew needed a much larger street location for the procession, which would involve hundreds of extras and a troop of cavalry, horses and gun carriages. The chosen location was Lacock in Wiltshire, much of which is built in a similar limestone to Bampton, with a layout of streets that look very much as they did 200 years ago. The historic feel of Lacock has made it a popular location for television and film production crews, and indeed the *Downton Abbey* crew briefly filmed there in the final series, transforming Church Street into a livestock market.

The parade was filmed in and around the high street in Lacock and the King's review of the troop was shot in playing fields nearby. Location manager Sparky Ellis and the production team met with the residents of the village to outline their plans for filming and to seek the residents' approval. Largely owned by the National Trust, Lacock has plenty of period features but there were still signs of modern life that needed to be removed for filming. Curtains or any modern window dressings needed to be taken away, as did residents' cars and twenty-first century street signs. Some items that were difficult to remove or cover up, such as TV aerials, could be erased digitally in post-production, but the crew, with the help of the residents, tried to remove as much as they could for filming.

KING GEORGE and QUEEN MARY

Simon Jones
Geraldine James

The actor Simon Jones was delighted to join the *Downton Abbey* cast, playing none other than King George V, his first regal role on screen. 'I've played the Emperor of Austria on stage, so that was my first taste of power, but this is my first king. Interestingly, when we were at Highclere shooting, I did seem to get quite a bit deference from the extras, almost as if George V had come back to life!'

Simon dutifully put in some background research on the King and realised that in order to recreate his look a beard was a must. In keeping with his naval upbringing, George grew a beard and moustache in his late teens, and kept them throughout his life. Previously clean-shaven, Simon started to grow a beard several weeks before the shoot and luckily it grew to almost the right shape (which was soon perfected with a little pruning from the hair-and-make-up team) – he was clearly destined for the role.

In building a picture of the man he was about to play, Simon also delighted in the odd revealing detail, one of which showed how much of a stickler the King was for protocol. 'King George thought it terribly bad taste to have a crease down the middle of trousers, with turn-ups at the bottom. It enraged him that his sons clearly didn't agree and I've seen a photo of him with his two sons, both of them wearing trousers with sharp creases down the middle and turn-ups.'

In the movie, we first glimpse the King and Queen as they sweep into the drive of Downton Abbey in a Daimler. Lined up at the entrance are the entire household, the Crawleys and family guests on the right and staff on the left. On hand during this key scene was the historical advisor Alastair Bruce, as he was during most of the filming process to answer the many questions that often crop up as scenes are shot. Simon explains one such moment, 'When we got out of the car and then crossed the gravel towards the house, it suddenly occurred to me, would I wipe my shoes on the doormat before going in? Alastair said absolutely not.'

One of the most challenging scenes for Simon was the parade in the village, during which the King inspects the Yorkshire Hussars. This was Simon's first scene of filming and he had to do the inspection on horseback, in front of the royal artillery, 300 extras and the whole cast and crew. 'That was quite a challenge – the last time I was on a horse was for a hunting scene in the period drama *Brideshead Revisited* and that was forty years ago! As a result, the production team had a double ready to take over, but it actually went okay and he wasn't needed. I think I earned my spurs that day!'

While at Downton, the King invites Bertie on a tour of the African colonies with his son the Prince of Wales. In reality, the King's relationship with his eldest son was strained by 1927 – George deeply disapproved of the Prince's bachelor lifestyle and his liking for fashionable clothes, clubs and cocktails while the Prince loathed his father's obsession with protocol and etiquette. In the film, the King believes Bertie could be just the man to provide a 'steadying influence' for his son while on a royal tour. It doesn't occur to him that Bertie might not want to be away when his first child is due, and it's only after Queen Mary explains the situation that the King agrees to release him from the obligation. The royal couple clearly have a good working relationship and her husband heeds the Queen's counsel when needed, much to the relief of Bertie and Edith.

Queen Mary is a great support to her husband. As Queen, she plays her part well; she is gracious to everyone at Downton and is kindly dismissive of Molesley's odd behaviour at dinner, knowing what a strange effect the presence of royalty can have on people.

'We had lots of pictorial references for the King so we could look at his outfits and their finer detail, from the kind of watch chain and cufflinks he wore to the type of stiff collar he favoured and his cravats. The cut of his trousers and the way he wore them was important – he disapproved of having a pressed seam – so we made sure we prepared and ironed his suits the right way.'

**Anna Robbins,
costume designer**

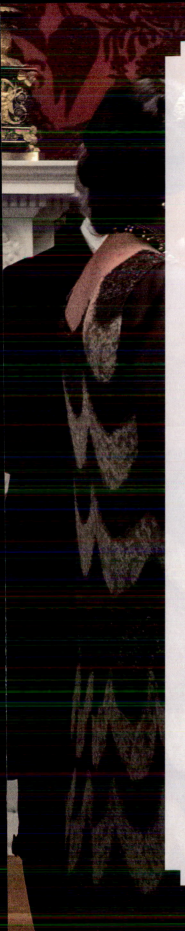

The visit to Yorkshire gives the Queen a chance to see her daughter, Princess Mary, about whom she is clearly worried, particularly as her son-in-law, Lord Lascelles, seems to absent himself from every family occasion.

The actor, Geraldine James, was admittedly chuffed to be asked to play the role and rose to the challenge wonderfully, almost magically transforming into Queen Mary.

'I don't think I was very good at being queen-like at first,' says Geraldine in a typically self-effacing way. 'We had an expert on hand who had to keep telling me not to walk so fast. "You must be stately and slow." So I had to rein myself in as I do tend to whizz about a bit.'

Added to this, there were many formalities that Geraldine needed to keep in mind when playing the Queen, not least when addressing servants. 'When the King and I leave Downton Abbey, the servants all line up to say goodbye. I'm trying to be gracious and look down the line to thank them, and Jim Carter [Carson] had to remind me that the servants couldn't look at the Queen but rather had to keep their eyes at knee height. I didn't realise just how distant royalty was, which took some getting used to.'

While Queen Mary could look rather severe in photographs, she was popular with the crowds and did a lot of charity work, so Geraldine was keen to give her a hint of humanity. 'Unlike her husband, she was cultured and loved going to the theatre and I wondered if she felt like a bit of outsider and slightly out of place. I liked that element of her being a little bit out of her depth at those huge dinner parties.'

At the same time, Geraldine was aware that George and Mary knew exactly how to play the role of King and Queen, a thought that struck her when she was sitting in the Daimler and giving the royal wave. 'In a sense you are being what people expect you to be. They don't necessarily want to see the inner person, they just want you to be King and Queen, smiling, accepting little gifts, and the like.' In the movie, the Queen is clearly conscious of the role she must play and is determined to keep up appearances at the village parade, insisting to her daughter that they must only discuss her marital problems in private.

'Queen Mary's look is well documented. She had a bit of a monster hair-do, a very tight wave that was kind of piled on top of her head in a rather unflattering way and which didn't really change much, other than the colour, as she got older. We went for a slightly more steely-grey for her hair as it suited Geraldine's skin tone.'

Nosh Oldham,
hair and make-up designer

In the presence of royalty, gentlemen were required to match the King's dress where appropriate. For the film this meant the male cast could have more changes than the women – creating plenty of work for the wardrobe department.

At the parade we see the King in his scarlet field marshal full dress uniform with full-sized medals and a cocked bicorne hat. He also wears the Most Noble Order of the Garter Breast Star; the Most Honourable Order of the Bath Breast Star; the Lesser George on his garter sash; and the Royal Victorian Chain at his neck.

When he arrives at Downton the King wears a tweed suit but for the tea after the parade he changes to a non-ceremonial blue serge frock coat, with medal ribbons. Robert follows suit while the non-uniformed gentlemen wear morning suits.

There were fifty-two elements to the King's costume, made up of his clothes, medals, boots, hats and other accessories, all of which had to be made. There were so many that the wardrobe department had to make spreadsheets for them all and tick them off as they went along.

'The gown that we made for the Queen for the ball has a skirt made from a silver lamé that actually belonged to Queen Mary. I had found some 1920s metallic lace as a starting point and John Bright added a piece of beaded cobwebbed lace that formed the sleeve. The whole piece came together really well – it was a career highlight for me.'

**Anna Robbins,
costume designer**

At the ball, Queen Mary wears the sash of the Order of the Garter, a diamond garter star and a diamond garter on her arm.

The Order of the Garter (which dates back to 1348) is the most prestigious order of chivalry, limited to the sovereign, the Prince of Wales and various chosen royal members, as well as no more than twenty-four living people appointed by the monarch on the advice of the government. The 'garter' is a piece of clothing worn either around the left calf by knights or around the left arm by ladies, with the motto 'Honi soit qui mal y pense' – Middle French for 'Shame on him who thinks ill of it'.

Pinned on her front the Queen has the Order of the Crown of India, the Royal Order of Victoria and Albert and the Royal Family Order, bestowed on her by her father-in-law along with other female members of the royal family and considered more a personal memento than a formal decoration.

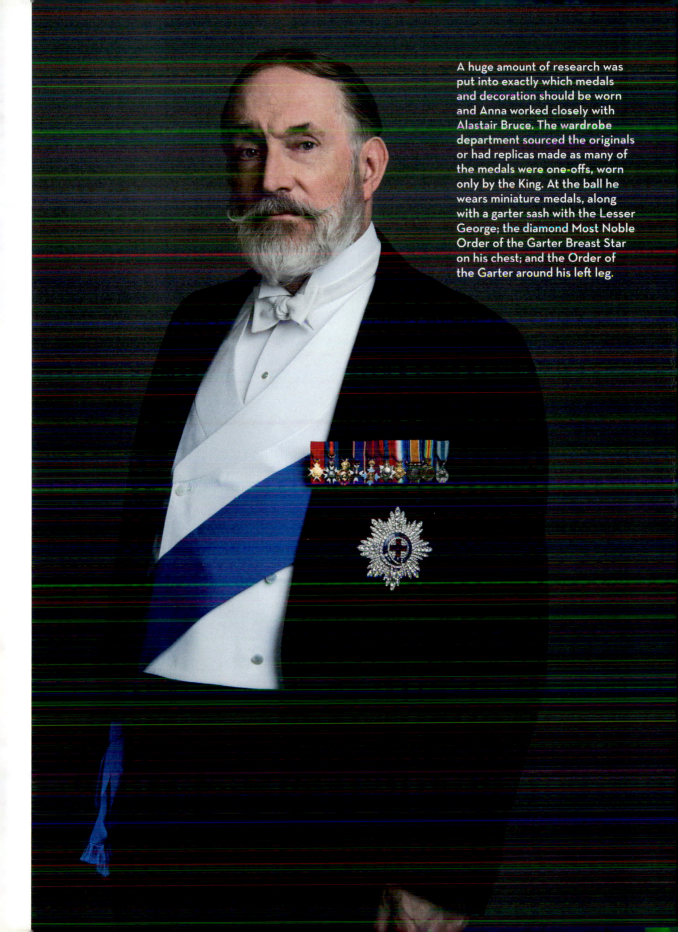

A huge amount of research was put into exactly which medals and decoration should be worn and Anna worked closely with Alastair Bruce. The wardrobe department sourced the originals or had replicas made as many of the medals were one-offs, worn only by the King. At the ball he wears miniature medals, along with a garter sash with the Lesser George; the diamond Most Noble Order of the Garter Breast Star on his chest; and the Order of the Garter around his left leg.

The King's Daimler

Cars are an increasingly common sight in *Downton Abbey*, as private ownership of motor cars steadily grew in the years after the First World War. In the 1920s, William R. Morris introduced to the UK the American techniques of mass-production to manufacture more affordable cars; at the same time his main British competitor, Herbert Austin, was producing the Austin Twenty, which proved to be one of the most popular cars of the day.

In the film, the King and Queen arrive at Downton in a Daimler, this particular model a 20HP limousine. King George's father, Edward VII, had favoured Daimler motor cars, having first ridden in one in 1896. The cars were manufactured under licence from Daimler in Germany and were awarded their first Royal Warrant as suppliers to the royal household in 1902. Daimler also supplied cars to various other royal families around the world, from Spain and Sweden to Malaysia and India. King George V continued patronage of the Daimler and it wasn't until the late 1940s that the royal family started to use Rolls-Royces and Bentleys as well. Daimlers are still used by the British royal family today.

Production designer Donal Woods and his production team wanted to source an exact version of the car that George V himself would have used. The car is painted in the royal colours of black and maroon, and the team added the royal standard above the windscreen and even recreated the mascot on the bonnet, featuring Britannia sitting on a globe (a mascot still used by the current Prince of Wales, Prince Charles, on his Rolls-Royce).

The Real King George and Queen Mary

Throughout the period in which the drama is set, King George V and Queen Mary have ruled as the heads of state, the King succeeding his father, King Edward VII, in 1910. As King and Queen Consort, as well as Emperor and Empress of India, their reign has encompassed the war years and the turbulent post-war period of the 1920s. The royal couple are popular with the crowds and well-versed in the public duties of monarchy.

During much of George's early life there was little expectation that he would be king. He was born in 1865, during the reign of his grandmother Queen Victoria, and it was assumed that his elder brother, Prince Albert Victor (known by the family as Eddy), would inherit the throne. All was to change in 1892, when Eddy unexpectedly died from influenza just after his twenty-eighth birthday, and George became king-in-waiting when his father assumed the throne in 1901.

Just six weeks before his death, Eddy had been betrothed to Princess Mary of Teck. Deemed by Queen Victoria as a suitable candidate for royal marriage, Mary had agreed to marry the Queen's rather wayward grandson. George's sudden promotion in the royal hierarchy hastened the need for him, too, to find a wife and the Queen urged him to ask for Princess Mary's hand in marriage.

They were married in the summer of 1893 at the Chapel Royal in St James's Palace, London.

Mary of Teck was born at Kensington Palace in London in 1867 and grew up in England. Typically for a British royal, she was of German blood, the only daughter of Francis, the Duke of Teck, a member of the royal house of Wuttemberg (a former German state), and Princess Mary Adelaide of Cambridge, granddaughter of King George III and Queen Victoria's first cousin. Mary was known by the family as 'May', after the month of her birth, although as Queen Consort she chose to be called Mary.

Like many royal brides before and after, Mary found her new in-laws rather distant and unwelcoming. Nonetheless, George proved himself to be a loyal and loving (albeit dominating) husband, and the couple remained devoted to each other, the marriage a strong alliance on which George's popularity as monarch rested.

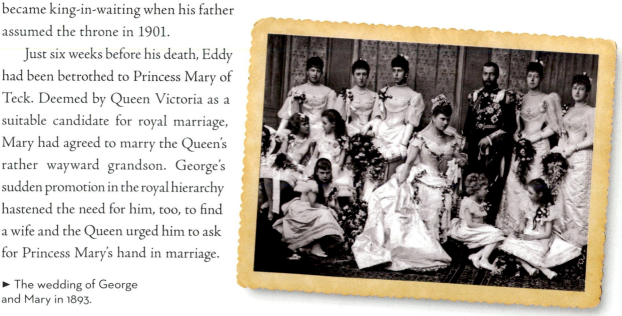

▶ The wedding of George and Mary in 1893.

▲ King George V and family at Abergeldie Castle, 1906. Left to right: George, Princess Mary, Queen Mary holding Prince John, Prince Henry (seated), Prince George, Prince Edward and Prince Albert.

From the age of twelve, largely at the insistence of his father, George received a naval education. From 1879, he and his brother served for three years on HMS *Bacchante*, touring colonies of the British Empire across the globe. George continued to serve in the Royal Navy, sailing in the Mediterranean and North American waters and received his first independent command in 1889. His naval career abruptly ended when his brother died, but his early years on the quarterdeck would have a lasting influence. Like his father, he was obsessed with protocol, punctuality and uniform, while his lack of academic schooling made him mistrustful of high culture and the creative arts.

George also shared with his father an obsession with hunting game birds, and shot thousands on the Sandringham estate in Norfolk. There the comparisons end, as George was adamant he would conduct himself in a very different way to his father. Edward VII entertained on a lavish scale, gambled excessively and had a string of mistresses throughout his life. George's mother, Princess Alexandra, was forced to accept her husband's infidelities, focusing her energies instead on doting on her five children (not least George, to whom she wrote when he was in command of a gunboat 'with a great big kiss for your lovely little face').

George preferred a quiet life as a country gentleman, initially living at the modest York Cottage on the Sandringham estate, where he also developed (alongside his love of shooting things) a love of stamp collecting. Mary was better educated than her husband, having been taught at home by a governess and her mother, and having travelled in Europe and lived for a short while in Florence. There she was able to visit museums and art galleries. Well read, she was fluent in French, German and English, and with artistic taste and intellect, she acknowledged that George 'knew nothing about pictures or history' or any foreign language, and she found his obsessions with shooting and yachting a little baffling.

Six children followed – Edward, Albert, Mary, Henry, George and John – all of them put into the care of nannies, as was common practice in the period. When her children were very young, Mary seemed a detached mother, certainly by today's modern sensibilities, failing to notice for three years the physical ill-treatment meted out by one nanny to her two elder sons. There was, nonetheless, a fun-loving, caring side to Mary, not perhaps seen in public – she taught her children history and music, and was greatly distressed at having to leave them for many months to tour the Empire in 1901. The future Edward VIII would write fondly of his mother in his memoirs (although he would also remark after her death that the fluids in her veins were 'icy cold as they are now in death'.)

During the ten years of his father's reign, George toured British colonies overseas with his wife and they were involved extensively in welfare and charity work. George was also given wide access to state papers, which he viewed with Mary as he valued her counsel. As wife to the future King, Mary understood that her prime task was to support her husband and thus the Crown. The pair seemed a solid and effective partnership in public and Mary provided George with the comfort and assurance he needed.

On succeeding the throne in 1910, King George immediately faced difficulties politically as Lord Asquith's Liberal government attempted to curtail the power of the House of Lords. The country at large was showing signs of division as trades unions grew, and dockers, railwaymen and coal miners went on strike. Fearing that such unrest could rock the political system, and the monarchy with it, the King was encouraged to meet the people and to tour the country visiting towns, villages and workplaces.

The country was to face even harder challenges when war broke out in 1914. As monarch and commander-in-chief of the armed forces, George was aware of the role he needed to play in uniting the country as a strong and stable figurehead. Court rituals at Buckingham Palace and shooting at Sandringham were immediately suspended and George and Mary embarked upon hundreds of royal visits, visiting hospitals, munitions factories and dockyards. The King increasingly relied on the Queen's support and advice as they both toured the Empire and attended royal engagements. He made at least 400 trips to see British and Imperial troops at home and on the Western Front (badly injuring his hip when he was thrown from his horse in

► King George V (front right), at the Trench Warfare School, Helfaut, France during the First World War, 7 July, 1917.

▲ King George V and Queen Mary visit the Canbury Park Road airplane factory.

France), while Mary was involved with many charitable institutions, enlisting the help of her daughter Princess Mary, and visiting wounded servicemen up and down the country.

In 1917, in a bid to distance himself from the German Kaiser Wilhelm II, his first cousin and now enemy of the country, King George changed the name of the royal house from the Germanic-sounding Saxe-Coburg-Gotha to Windsor, and any noble relatives were also required to relinquish German titles. In the same year, as monarchies across Europe toppled, fearing a similar uprising against the British monarchy, George vetoed the offer of asylum to another cousin, Tsar Nicholas II, who had been overthrown as a result of the Russian Revolution. To the shock of King George, the Tsar and his family were eventually shot and bayoneted by Bolsheviks in 1918.

The trauma of war would be felt for many years after the armistice, and was still a raw memory for those living in 1927. The country had suffered huge loss of life, memorials to the dead were erected throughout the country, and Britain was impoverished, owing millions to the USA. The monarchy in Britain had survived but the majority of King George's royal relatives in Europe – in Austria, Germany, Greece, Spain and Russia – had fallen. The British Empire, so prized by George, was similarly showing signs of fragmentation as dominions demanded more say in how they were run, the gradual move towards independence unavoidable.

In Britain, many of the settled, unchallenged patterns evident during the Edwardian era were

► Tsar Nicholas II and George V in 1913.

◄ 6 May 1926: A bus leaving the garage under police protection during the General Strike.

was fully resumed at Buckingham Palace and Windsor and shooting was back on the schedule at Sandringham.

In 1926, industrial decline, worsening unemployment and social division led to the 1926 General Strike (as alluded to by the King to Cora in the film). A dispute over conditions, wage cuts and dismissals in the coal-mining industry, followed by Stanley Baldwin breaking off negotiations with the Trade Union Congress (TUC), prompted the unions to strike. With some 1.7 million workers walking out, mainly in the transport and heavy industries, Britain was virtually at a standstill for nine days between 3 and 12 May 1926. While the King was in favour of measures to curb disorder, he was sympathetic to the strikers and advised Baldwin not to take too harsh a line with them, saying: 'Try living on their wages before you judge them.' Though the TUC would eventually give up in defeat, the General Strike showed the effect worker solidarity could have on the country.

King George was aware that Britain in the 1920s was changing, that the younger generation, like *Downton Abbey*'s Daisy, were no longer content with their lot in life, questioning the age-old values of deference and discipline, on which great houses like Downton Abbey and the monarchy rested. Life was changing – telephones, gramophones and hair-dryers had already arrived at Downton, and the refrigerator was now a permanent feature in the kitchen. Cinema was

increasingly under assault. The ruling classes, which had suffered disproportionate losses during the war, had lost political clout; the franchise had been extended in 1918 (and was about to be extended further in 1928) and the House of Lords had lost it political veto. Great estates, like Downton Abbey, were being put on the market and traditional class barriers had been weakened, as soldiers from all classes fought and died alongside each other.

Socialism was also on the rise and in 1924 King George invited Ramsay MacDonald to form the country's first Labour government. Although a natural Tory who loathed radical socialists, George was welcoming and conciliatory to the Labour government, which he hoped would steer a political middle path. It was short-lived though, as later that year the Conservatives were back in power under the helm of Stanley Baldwin and would remain so until 1929. Baldwin's government wanted to return to the stability of the pre-war years and King George was similarly keen to return to normality. As a result, court life experiencing something of a boom as Hollywood expanded its film-making in the 1920s, with the first 'talkie' film, *The Jazz Singer*, shown in Britain in 1928. The decade also brought in new styles of music and dance clubs were opening in cities across the country. Developments in transportation meant that motor cars were an increasingly common sight on the roads, and in 1927 Charles Lindbergh was able to make the first solo non-stop transatlantic flight, from New York to Paris.

Against this backdrop and on the advice of courtiers and the government, the royal couple continued touring the country, attending sporting events, schools, workplaces and industrial areas, all the while establishing the King's image as a churchgoer and decent family man, a king who was above the people but who could also share in his people's hopes and values. Queen Mary continued to staunchly support her husband throughout the difficult post-war years. Dressed in formal long dresses and toque hats, she could appear a little stiff and austere, but to others she seemed self-assured and calm at public engagements. Duty was her watchword and formality provided her with a kind of protective shield as she performed her role as loyal wife to the king.

Throughout the 1920s, the royal family carried out around 3,000 public engagements and also increased the number of royal ceremonial occasions, to include the wedding of Princess Mary to Lord Lascelles in 1922. Many of the royal visits and

ceremonies were filmed on newsreels and shown in the growing number of cinemas up and down the country, the King and Queen surprisingly comfortable and adept before the cameras.

Turbulent years lay ahead for the monarchy, not least with the succession of the Prince of Wales to the throne as King Edward VIII in 1936. His political leanings and playboy lifestyle, which so troubled the King and Queen, were of similar concern to the authorities, and his determination to marry an American divorcee would result in his abdication shortly after, his brother Albert succeeding him as King George VI. The monarchy, however, would weather the storm, King George and Queen Mary having sufficiently bolstered the institution to survive the crisis.

► George and Mary at the christening of Princess (later Queen) Elizabeth, 29 May 1926.

LADY BAGSHAW

Imelda Staunton

Accompanying the King and Queen when they arrive at Downton Abbey is a select retinue of staff, including the Queen's lady-in-waiting Maud Bagshaw. She's not exactly thrilled to be at Downton, having previously revealed to Queen Mary that she is a relation of the Crawleys and there is bad blood between the families.

The mystery deepens when we learn that Lord Grantham is in fact her nearest relation (her father was his great-uncle) and is the rightful heir to her estate, Brompton Park. However, she has chosen to cut herself off from the family and, much to Violet's indignation, it is believed she has chosen to deny Robert the inheritance.

The stage is thus set for a showdown between the Dowager Countess and Lady Bagshaw, a confrontation that Maud (not unsurprisingly) attempts to avoid during her stay with the Crawleys. The role required an actor who could match Violet in stature, and award-winning actor Imelda Staunton achieves this with aplomb. Director Michael Engler agrees: 'Lady Bagshaw has to be a formidable opponent to Violet, and we needed an actor who could hold her own, and Imelda of course did that very well.'

'I loved the role of Maud and it was great to play those really tense scenes with Maggie [Violet] and Penelope [Isobel],' says Imelda. 'We exchange some strong words – and certainly don't discuss hemlines or the weather.' It was a treat also for Imelda to spend the odd day with her real husband, Jim Carter, who plays Carson, 'We did have a couple of dinner scenes together, although he was largely at the other end of the room and he didn't serve me so much as a sherry!'

As well as her scenes with the original cast of *Downton Abbey*, Imelda appears for much of the film alongside Geraldine James, who plays Queen Mary. As lady-in-waiting, her character Maud must see to the Queen's every need. A lady-in-waiting was chosen from noble ranks and would largely be considered a personal assistant and companion to the Queen rather than a servant. She would generally travel with the Queen, attend public events, handle correspondence and see to the Queen's various needs, often as a trusted confidante. As such, Imelda needed to follow many protocols, so she found the historical advice given to her on set by Alastair Bruce invaluable. 'Alastair told me that as soon as the Queen stands, I must stand immediately,' Imelda explains, joking, 'I was at Geraldine's beck and call morning and night!'

Creating the costumes for Maud provided Anna Robbins with the opportunity to create quite a different look from any of the other characters. 'We had really good picture references for Queen Mary's ladies-in-waiting. A lady herself, her clothing would have been high quality and bespoke, and in accordance with royal protocol and propriety. We had a good early fitting with Imelda, looking at fabrics and colours that worked well with her skin tone and shapes that suited her. We put her in a beautiful velvet suit, with a blouse worn over the skirt, rather than tucked in, just to give a nod to the 1920s. Her hats were mainly wide-brimmed, rather than the more current cloche style – all a mixture of different influences.'

As the story unfolds, we discover that Lady Bagshaw's maid, Lucy, is in fact her own daughter, the result of a relationship with her deceased husband's army servant Jack Smith, unexpectedly conceived when Maud was thirty-nine. Such a scandal would have finished her in high society. To escape the ensuing uproar, Lady Bagshaw was forced to travel to America, before returning to England six months after her baby was born and taking up her position at the royal household.

Violet is enraged when she first learns that Lady Bagshaw is to leave her estate to Lucy, although when Violet learns of Maud's secret, the Dowager is, to Maud's surprise, understanding: 'Well,

Isobel: 'You must tell Violet at once.'

Maud: 'I couldn't.'

Isobel: 'You're wrong. As soon as she knows the truth, she'll fathom your plans and cease to fight you.'

who do you think I am? Some maiden aunt who never left the village?' Although it is clear that she won't be able to regain Brompton Park for Robert, Violet in no way sees this as a defeat. Instead she is mollified by the fact that Tom Branson and Lucy have struck up a romance — thereby putting him in the frame for the inheritance. By the time the royal party move on to Harewood, Maud has been welcomed back into the family.

LUCY SMITH

Tuppence Middleton

Lucy arrives with the royal entourage, as maid to Lady Bagshaw, the Queen's lady-in-waiting. It soon becomes apparent that Lady Bagshaw and her maid are unusually close, and their relationship may not be what it seems.

Lucy is in fact the secret daughter of Lady Bagshaw. She lived with her father, Jack Smith, until he died, when she was six years old. Lady Bagshaw then took her in as her 'maid'; anything of higher status would have aroused people's suspicions. Since the age of eighteen, Lucy has known the truth about her mother and the two have clearly developed a close bond.

New cast member Tuppence Middleton plays the role of Lucy Smith and was thrilled to be among such esteemed actors, coming also from a family of *Downton Abbey* fans. 'There was one day where I walked onto set and I was doing a scene with Maggie Smith and Imelda Staunton,' explains Tuppence, 'and I had to take a breath and try and take it all in – it was amazing to see both of them work and very exciting.'

Lucy's arrival at Downton also attracts the attention of Branson. Having snatched a few moments together, Lucy is interested in his rise from chauffeur to family member, as she will one day experience a similar rise in status when she inherits her mother's estate. There is clearly an attraction between the two, and when Lucy agrees to correspond with Tom, he leans in to kiss her. We later see them dancing on the terrace at the ball, clearly captivated by one another.

Lucy: 'I have such a feeling that you can understand what's going on inside my head when no one else does, or ever could.'

◄ 10 September 1927: The Royal Garden Party at Balmoral. From left to right are the Duke of York, King George V, the Duchess of York and Queen Mary. Princess Elizabeth, our future Queen, is in the pram.

for business or pleasure, was perfectly managed and was often met with great ceremony. In 1927, the year in which the movie is set, George V stayed at the Earl of Sefton's Abbeystead estate in Lancashire, where he had been shooting. From there, he travelled by train to Balmoral and was met by a guard of honour from the King's Guard of the 1st Battalion the Royal Scots, and the Lord Lieutenant of Aberdeenshire. On the same day, Queen Mary visited Princess Mary at Goldsborough; crowds cheered her as she left Harrogate Station. Five days later she journeyed up to Balmoral, where she was met with a similar degree of ceremony as the King.

obvious base for the tour. As the royals arrived, thousands lined the streets between Doncaster Station and Wentworth and a further 40,000 were waiting for them in the park. Their stay coincided with a major disaster at nearby Cadeby Colliery, which was to lead to the loss of ninety-one lives. After visiting other local collieries – the King even descending into the mine at Elsecar – the royal couple visited the site of the disaster, where some 80,000 people had assembled, witnessing the Queen in tears as she left the pit office.

The 1920s were still turbulent times, particularly after the Great Strike of 1926, which increased the need for the monarchy to get among the people. Every trip, whether it was

► Queen Mary visits Silverwood Colliery in Yorkshire in 1912.

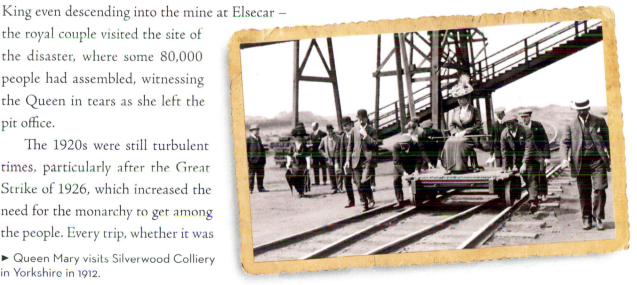

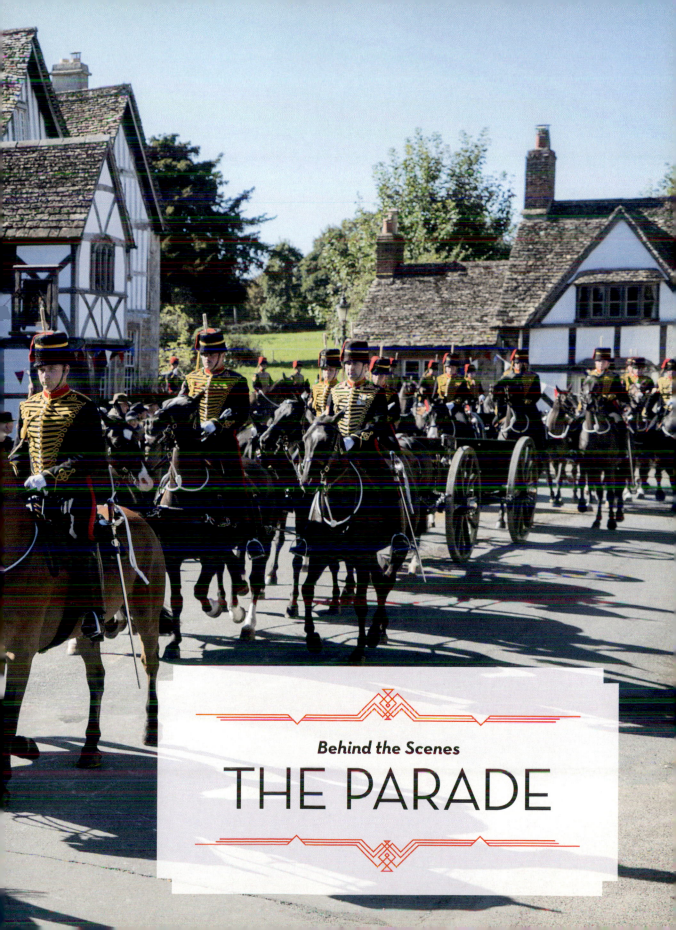

Behind the Scenes

THE PARADE

The Commanding Officer rides up
to the King, salutes with his sword and announces:
'Your Majesty, the Yorkshire Hussars
are formed up, ready and awaiting
your inspection.'

One of the most spectacular scenes in the *Downton Abbey* film is the parade of the Yorkshire Hussars in the village, followed by the King's inspection of the troops. It's a splendid sight, the yeomanry in ceremonial dress of gold and black in a stately procession of horses and gun carriages glinting in the sunshine. The streets are dressed in bunting and everyone is there, the royals and the Crawley family on a raised dais, the Downton staff and hundreds of villagers waving flags and cheering as the procession passes.

Filming such a scene, with around 300 extras and the main cast, a hundred crew members, along with the King's Troop Royal Horse Artillery and around sixty horses, including six teams of horses pulling First World War guns, is a complex undertaking. The production crew must carefully plan every aspect of the shoot, from sourcing and overseeing the huge number of people and horses involved, to dressing the streets, organising costume and make-up for all the extras, and overseeing the complex filming schedule during the four days of filming. Co-producer Mark Hubbard, who, with his team, handled much of the day-to-day management of the film, explains: 'We talked a lot about that scene as it really was a logistical challenge and quite a daunting thing to tackle. Luckily, the weather was glorious.'

Ben Smithard, the director of photography, who oversees cameras, lighting and the visual look of the film, agrees: 'The parade scene was the biggest sequence in the film and perhaps bigger than anything shot in the TV series. We spent four days in the village of Lacock, closing a whole street off for one day. We had three or four cameras, filming on the ground or on cranes, and the logistics really were tricky as so much could go wrong.'

Despite the hundreds of cast and crew that arrived for filming, not to mention the soldiers, horses and the countless trucks that accompany all film crews, life still had to go on in the village, particularly for its younger residents. Areas of the village were cordoned for filming but the production team had to work around the school situated on the high street, allowing for parents to drop off and pick up children at the beginning and end of the school day.

Dressing the whole *Downton* cast along with hundreds of extras is a huge challenge for the wardrobe department. In order to dress and process so many people, Anna Robbins had to draft in extra people to help over the two days of filming. Beginning before the sun was up, they started dressing people with military precision, making sure everyone from the working-class spectators in their Sunday best to the aristocrats on the dais were looking their best. 'It's always a treat to see some of the Downton staff out of their uniforms and in daywear,' says Anna.

The parade scene features the Yorkshire Hussars, a volunteer yeoman cavalry unit of the British Army, first formed in 1794 to defend Britain against a French invasion. Cavalry units such as

these harken back to a former age of warfare, their uniforms unchanged since the 1800s, an echo of an older world. Nonetheless, it is only right that the public should support them in such a parade, as, like other cavalry units, volunteer members of the Yorkshire Hussars played their part in the First World War, fighting in France, at Ypres, Loos, and Arras, among other battles, some remaining on the Western Front until the end of the war. In the face of mechanised warfare, however, it was clear the days of the cavalry were numbered, although some regiments, like the Yorkshire Hussars, were kept on as horsed units for a little while longer.

To re-enact the procession of the Yorkshire Hussars, the production team brought in the King's Troop Royal Horse Artillery, a mounted unit of the British Army that is used to fire royal salutes to mark the grand occasions of state. The origins of the unit date back to the eighteenth century, but its current form evolved in 1946 following the phasing out of the cavalry and the mechanisation of horse-drawn artillery. King George VI had requested that a troop of artillery should be retained to fire salutes on state occasions, dressed in traditional ceremonial uniform. Today these soldiers, who are all trained to drive teams of horses pulling field guns, fire salutes at the Trooping of the Colour to celebrate the Queen's official birthday. In 1997, members of the King's Troop pulled a gun carriage carrying the coffin of

Diana, Princess of Wales, while members of the royal family walked behind.

Mark Hubbard says: 'We decided to go with the King's Troop as their uniforms and equipment are right for the period. They know how to march in processions and exactly what they are doing, which made the whole process much easier.'

For the members of the Royal Horse Artillery, the experience of filming was an enjoyable one and the set-up similar to being in a real parade. The horses were transported in nine lorries from Woolwich in south-east London to the filming location in Lacock in Wiltshire, 140 miles away. A make-shift camp was set up in a field just at the end of the high street, made up of stables for the horses and a number of marquees containing sleeping quarters, showers, catering, costumes and equipment. Sparky Ellis, the location manager

for *Downton Abbey*, helped to organise 'horse base', as the film's crew called it: 'With the help of a company who set up equestrian events around the country, we created what was effectively a mini-village on the edge of Lacock. We had the whole thing up for just under two weeks, then collapsed it all down and the circus moved on. It was a huge operation.'

Once filming started, riders and horses needed to be flexible about timings and were generally alerted when they were needed by trumpet calls across the camp. The shoot involved long days of waiting around, interspersed with short bursts of action – a little like being at war, some of the soldiers joked, but without getting shot at!

The commander of the King's Troop not only had to lead the unit around the village and then line them up, but he also had to address the King as part of the ceremony. As the real Commanding Officer of the troop, Major Harry Wallace RHA,

was obviously not a professional actor, producer Mark Hubbard had to go to the trade union Equity for dispensation to cast him in this small speaking role. As Mark recalls, 'I explained that I couldn't get an actor to lead sixty horses and six gun carriages, it really had to be this specific person! Equity understood the situation, thankfully. The Major did a great job, which isn't surprising really as he does this kind of thing in front of our Queen!'

The parade included six gun teams, each 60-feet in length, with six horses pulling guns and limber (carriages) weighing 1.5 tonnes. Each gun dates back to 1904 and all saw action on the Western Front during the First World War.

The only modifications made to the soldiers' uniforms were the replacement of the current Queen's insignia with those of George V and medals from the era. Otherwise the ceremonial uniform was unchanged as it is based on the 1860s Royal Horse Artillery uniform worn in the Crimea Campaign.

MAJOR CHETWODE

Stephen Campbell Moore

At the beginning of the film, a mysterious figure emerges from the steam at King's Cross and boards the train that's carrying the letter from Buckingham Palace to Downton Abbey. We see the same man in the village of Downton, as he checks in at the local pub.

When the figure announces himself as 'Major Chetwode' and begins to question Branson about whether he supports the King and Queen, we suspect he is some sort of agent of the Crown. Branson assumes Chetwode knows his history and has come to check on whether he's intending to sabotage the royal visit, for the sake of his homeland, Ireland.

It emerges, however, that it is Chetwode who is fighting for the republican cause. In his room we see him pull a revolver from his suitcase; he plans to assassinate the King. Fortunately as the Major raises the revolver at the parade, Branson, who has followed him through the crowd, manages to push him to the ground, and Mary, who is close behind, kicks the gun out of his hand, before two plain-clothed policemen pin him down to arrest him.

When Julian Fellowes was writing the script, Gareth Neame suggested that the character of Chetwode be influenced by members of the British establishment of the era who became sympathetic to the Irish cause. One such individual was Erskine Childers, author of what is often regarded as the first spy novel, *The Riddle of the Sands*. A former House of Commons employee, Childers devoted his later life to the support of Irish Home Rule, eventually being executed for treason in Dublin in 1922.

Mary: 'It's so strange. He seemed so English.'

Branson: 'And so he was. A pillar of the establishment, until the notion of Irish independence took him over to the other side.'

Stephen Campbell Moore, who plays Chetwode, jokes that, while wrestling with Allen Leech on the ground might not get him any fan mail, he did have fun playing a character that viewers hadn't met before: 'You can't quite put your finger on what he's up to and why he's so interested in Branson. He literally pops in and pops out and there's an element of mystery to him.'

When he read the script, Stephen was also struck by the film's unconventional storyline: 'For me it's unusual as a film and brings together lots of different characters. I think it's a pleasure to see such an expansive film unfold through the eyes of these characters, instead of through one hero, and one point of view.'

Despite being a new character on the *Downton* set, Stephen was immediately welcomed by his fellow actors. He also felt that director Michael Engler contributed to the friendly environment on set: 'A director has to create an atmosphere where people can work at their best, and Michael does that. For me he's great because he doesn't give long, convoluted notes, he says things quite simply and you have total trust in him. He's got a really good sense of where the story is going, and when a director imbues you with confidence and knows their subject matter, then it's always a good experience.'

Free Ireland

The struggle for the control of Ireland was still a bitter issue in 1927, so much so that the seemingly establishment figure of Major Chetwode is motivated to take up the republican cause, risking all to assassinate the King. British involvement in Ireland had for many years caused deep resentment and Irish republicans were vehemently opposed to an Anglo–Irish treaty that in 1921 had led to the partition of Ireland into Northern Ireland and the independent Irish Free State (the former Southern Ireland).

Violent clashes between the Irish Republican Army (IRA) and British paramilitary forces (the 'Black and Tans') had led to the agreement, and George V himself (under the protection of some 10,000 troops) opened the Ulster parliament in June 1921, where in a moving speech he urged all Irishmen 'to forgive and forget'. It was not to be – instead the treaty served to divide nationalists into those who favoured it and those who were opposed to the dominion status of the Irish Free State, which was still part of the British Empire with the British monarch its head of state.

Many saw the treaty as a betrayal of the Irish Republic which had been proclaimed in 1916 during the Easter Rising, and vowed to sever remaining ties with Britain. Tom Branson admitted that when he and Sybil moved back to Dublin in 1919 he had attended rallies by the IRA and had been part of the movement involved in the arson of Anglo–Irish homes in Ireland. The sight of families losing their houses, however, proved too much for Tom, and he and Sybil, who was then pregnant, moved back to England and Downton Abbey.

In Ireland, civil war ensued between June 1922 and May 1923, ending in victory for those who favoured the treaty. But the conflict left Irish society divided for generations, and King George provided an obvious target for those who, like Chetwode, shared the view that Ireland could not be free with 'the bloody Crown around its neck'.

AT HOME IN SHEPPERTON

Much of the action in the movie – the frenzied preparations for the royal visit and the showdown between the Downton staff and royal servants – takes place below stairs. Filming for many of these scenes was done at Shepperton Studios in Surrey, where a large set was built to represent the downstairs area of Downton, along with other key interiors seen in the film.

As in many other stately homes, most of the below-stairs rooms no longer exist in their original form at Highclere, and if they do, they are often difficult to light for filming. For that reason, the art directors have always built sets for the servants' area of Downton Abbey, designing rooms that are historically accurate and appear authentic on screen, but can also accommodate a large cast, crew and their equipment.

The result is an interlocking structure of rooms, complete with stairs that appear to lead to up to the family rooms and corridors that are wide enough to allow the staff to rush past each other while cameras and crew film them. 'The set is designed for flow and movement as below stairs is always busy and hectic,' explains production designer Donal Woods. All the rooms have open ceilings to allow for lights and cameras, although there is a solidity to the structure, with stone flags on the floors, and it retains the intimacy of a working country house.

For the movie, the set-build at Shepperton was bigger than the one created at Ealing Studios for the television series. The original servant areas were recreated in meticulous detail and extra rooms were added. All of Downton Abbey's bedrooms were rebuilt and filmed at Shepperton, along with the interior of Mr Carson and Mrs Hughes' cottage and the village post office. Extra rooms were also added to the servants' quarters, including a new wine cellar, a silver room, servery and more servant bedrooms.

The kitchen was built to look exactly the same, although special touches were added here and there by Gina Cromwell's set decoration team so that even more pots and pans gleam in the light. The dimensions of the kitchen were also a little different, as Lesley Nicol, who plays Mrs Patmore, noticed: 'I know that kitchen so well I did spot that, but otherwise coming back on set was like coming back home.'

For new members of the cast, like Susan Lynch, who plays the Queen's dresser Miss Lawton, walking on to the set at Shepperton was an almost magical feeling: 'The moment I walked into the kitchen, just seeing the way it had been lit, I could really see the work that had been put in. It looked like a picture.'

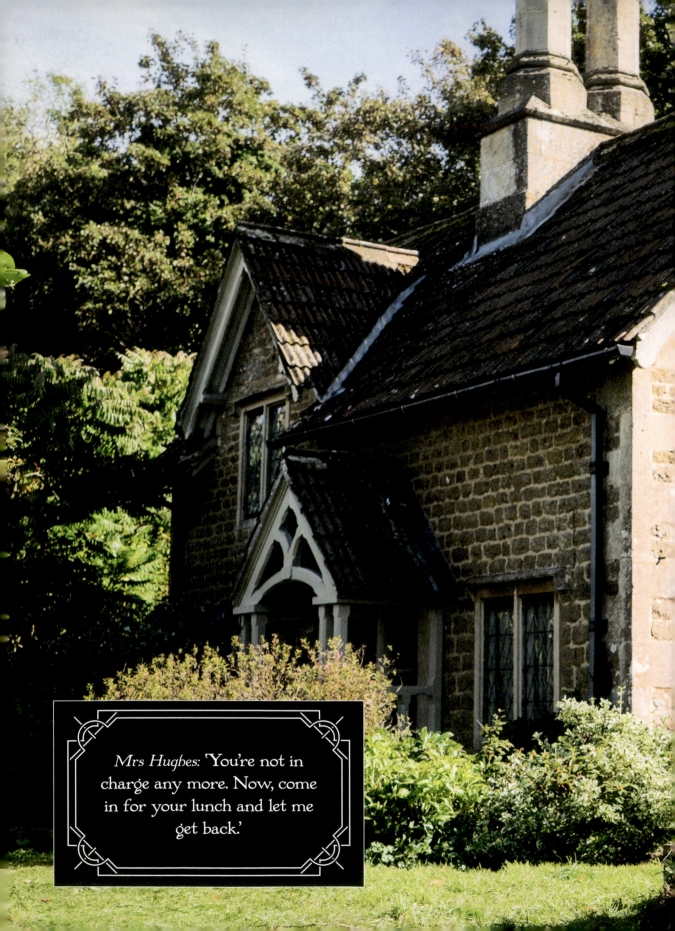

Mrs Hughes: 'You're not in charge any more. Now, come in for your lunch and let me get back.'

MR CARSON and MRS HUGHES

Jim Carter
Phyllis Logan

By 1927, Downton Abbey's long-serving butler Carson has retired, and we see him tending to his vegetable garden at the cottage he now shares with his new wife, Downton Abbey's housekeeper Elsie Hughes. For actor Jim Carter, the film was also an opportunity for him to go in for the occasional day's filming with his real wife Imelda Staunton, although as they didn't share many scenes this didn't happen often.

Carson's loyalty to the Crawley family still runs deep and it takes very little to encourage him to return to Downton – particularly as it's at the personal request of Mary, who has doubts that his successor, Mr Barrow, can cope with a royal visit. As Mrs Hughes reminds us, Carson has never been able to refuse her.

While Carson is itching to don his butler's livery again, the knowledge that the King and Queen are to visit Downton Abbey is also a huge draw. He knows what an honour it is for the family to receive the royal couple and he shares Mary's doubts about Mr Barrow too. Jim Carter explains: 'Carson is a fervent royalist and supporter of the status quo. In an earlier TV season, he nearly burst with pride when a high-born duke pays a visit. To be in the same room as the King would simply be the greatest moment of his life.'

Almost as if his destiny is calling him, Carson heroically takes charge of his former domain at Downton. 'I felt I should go where I

could do the most good,' he responds to the Dowager when she asks him about his return. After a gap of three years, Jim was equally pleased to be back on the *Downton Abbey* set – both Shepperton studios for scenes below stairs and the 'very nice' office of Highclere Castle, as he calls it, for scenes with the Crawley family.

His return means working once more alongside Mrs Hughes (who even though she married him is never known as Mrs Carson). Decent to the core, she maintains a kind and steadying hand at the house – the 'intelligent, moral leader of below stairs' as writer Julian Fellowes puts it. While she is loyal to her employers she isn't quite as enthralled by them as Mr Carson, and as such provides the perfect foil to her husband's more conservative tendencies. Like Phyllis Logan who plays her, Mrs Hughes has a Scottish background and is not afraid to speak her mind when the need arises.

Mrs Hughes' sense of fairness is seriously tested when the royal servants begin to take over Downton Abbey. Having overseen the

exhaustive cleaning of the house – 'I want every surface in this house to gleam and sparkle' – she, like all the Downton staff, is pushed aside when the royal household arrive. At first she tries to take a measured approach to the invasion, but their behaviour proves too much to bear, particularly after a showdown with the royal housekeeper, Mrs Webb. As Phyllis explains: 'While we're daunted by the prospect of a royal visit, we're also miffed to discover they've brought their entire entourage with them and we're obviously surplus to requirements.'

Playing an active part in the below stairs' insurrection, Mrs Hughes proves to be more than a match for her nemesis Mrs Webb. Throughout it all, our sympathies are, of course, firmly on the side of the redoubtable Mrs Hughes.

Mrs Hughes: 'Mr Carson, this is your destiny. You know as much, and so do I. Now accept it proudly and walk into that room with your head held high.'

Mr Wilson: 'Mr Carson, you are a retired servant in a minor, provincial house, serving an undistinguished family.'

We also see Mr Carson butting heads with the self-important Mr Wilson, the King's Page of the Backstairs. Unnerved to no longer be calling the shots, Carson is reluctantly swept up in the servants' plot to regain a hold on their domain. He plays his part in the uprising admirably and ultimately, of course, the Downton staff survive the royal visit.

It is left to Mrs Hughes and Carson to utter the final lines of the film as they take their leave of the great house, a moment certainly captured in Jim's memory: 'We came out just as it was getting dark. There was a beautiful sky behind Highclere Castle and as the cameras pulled away, there it is standing resplendent in its own cinematic timewarp.' It was clearly a good day at the office.

'On set, Jim is like the father of the downstairs team. Just like [my character] Andy, I felt that if he was there, everything was fine, we could just follow his lead.'

Michael Fox

Violet: 'How comforting to see you here, Carson. What prompted you to take up the flaming sword again?'

Downton Abbey descends into a frenzy of cleaning in preparation for the royal visit. Mrs Hughes must oversee the whole process and the family is reliant on the downstairs staff to put on a good show. Mrs Hughes already has exacting standards but everything must literally gleam and sparkle for the King and Queen, and her preparations are thorough and meticulous. Curtains are taken down, rugs are taken up, maids make beds, scrub and polish, while gardeners clip the hedges and mow the lawns.

Before the King and Queen arrive, everything must be checked and checked again. When King George V came to stay in 1912 at Wentworth Woodhouse (the filming location for the ballroom scene), the housekeeper had to prepare everything for the imminent arrival. The thirty-six guest bedrooms needed to be thoroughly cleaned, beds made, wardrobes and drawers dusted and freshly lined, stationery supplies and full inkstands placed in each room. All around the house there were vases of flowers and bowls of potpourri to release pleasant aromas into the air. A further forty bedrooms were also prepared for the guests' valets, ladies' maids and chauffeurs.

As Mrs Hughes tells the staff: 'We've only a few days left so I spoke to Her Ladyship and she's agreed our normal rules should be suspended. We won't clean a room if a family member is using it, but otherwise all restrictions are lifted. No detail should be left undone, however small.'

MR BARROW

Robert James-Collier

Thomas Barrow has finally made it as butler of Downton Abbey, but he is one of the first to suffer from the turmoil of the royal visit. Mary, who is clearly in a bit of a spin herself, begins to doubt whether Mr Barrow can manage the preparations, particularly when she finds him in a trance over the cleaning of the house silver. Much to Thomas's surprise, Mary calls in Mr Carson to replace him. Robert James-Collier, who plays Mr Barrow, explains: 'Out of nowhere Mary usurps him and pulls the rug from under his feet. And they wheel Carson back out of nowhere, with his creaky joints, and he becomes butler.'

Thomas is predictably furious at this turn of events, openly so to Lord Grantham as he surrenders his position for the duration of the visit. While Mary queries whether Mr Barrow is to be sacked, Robert is more interested to see that Thomas is a man of principle, having in the past questioned his integrity. Once ruthlessly ambitious and at times unkind, Barrow has had a difficult journey in life, coping with a sexuality that has alienated him from others and brought him to the very brink of despair. This in turn exposed his vulnerabilities and he vowed to reform his behaviour.

Thomas's hopes of friendship are raised when he meets the affable valet of the King, Richard Ellis, one of the advance party of servants who arrive at Downton. There is clearly a spark of connection between the two and it's apparent Thomas yearns to meet a kindred spirit, as Robert James-Collier says: 'For once, Barrow can have a proper chat with someone and get to be himself without hiding who he really is.'

Relieved of his duties at Downton Abbey, Thomas is free to take up Mr Ellis's offer of a night out. He heads to York and while waiting for Mr Ellis at a pub he catches the eye of a man who takes him to an underground nightclub. There, Thomas is stunned to see men openly dancing together but soon joins in. When the club is raided by the police and Thomas is among the men arrested, it is Richard Ellis who comes to his rescue, trading on his royal connections.

It's a scene that reminds us of the predicament that men like Thomas faced. Homosexuality was illegal in Britain, and remained so until 1967, with marriage between same-sex couples legalised

only as recently as 2014. In 1927, those convicted of homosexuality could be sentenced to imprisonment and hard labour, although the vagueness of the law allowed the police considerable discretion over what constituted an offence. Even more devastating than a prison sentence was society's disapproval, meaning men were forced to cover up their sexuality.

As a result, Mr Ellis advises Thomas to be more cautious in the future and there's an increasing connection between the two men. Thomas has at last found someone he can confide in – 'I feel I've finally found a friend' – and Mr Ellis also seems relieved that they can talk simply as 'two ordinary blokes'. Just before Richard Ellis leaves, the two men briefly kiss and Ellis gives Thomas a key ring as a keepsake. It's a gift that, we hope, might lead to a possible future reunion.

Thomas: 'Will they ever see it our way?'

Ellis: 'I don't know. Fifty years ago, who'd have thought man could fly?'

It is the butler's job to oversee the cleaning of the silver – of which Downton Abbey has a vast quantity – as the best pieces need to be put on display for special guests. Silver needs careful handling and gloves must be worn, as hands leave oils and moisture on the surface which can mark and tarnish the metal. Butlers could spend an inordinate amount of time cleaning silver and plate, leaving their hands as 'hard as boards' afterwards.

Whereas silverware was largely the province of the butler, footmen took charge of candlesticks, lamps, and other small items of furniture.

Valets and ladies' maids were responsible for more intimate or expensive items belonging to their masters and mistresses, such as ornaments, clothing and shoes. We frequently see the Downton staff repairing items of clothes or cleaning and buffing shoes in the boot room.

THOMAS'S NIGHT OUT

Thomas: 'I can't believe this.
I've never seen anything like it.'
Webster: 'There's a first time for everything.'

When Thomas's new acquaintance Chris Webster (played by Perry Fitzpatrick) takes him to the illegal nightclub Turton's, Thomas is amazed by what he sees, but soon throws himself into the intoxicating atmosphere of the club, drinking and dancing with Webster, until they're suddenly confronted by policemen. Everyone is promptly arrested – one policeman

exclaiming, 'Right! Gather your things. You're coming with us, you dirty perverts,' – and they are all taken down to the police station.

The pub scene was actually filmed 200 miles south of York, in Hammersmith, London, in an original Edwardian pub that is now closed to the drinking public and used solely as a film and TV location. Turton's nightclub was shot back in

Yorkshire, in a disused cotton mill in Keighley while a conservation area of Victorian warehouses in nearby Bradford, known as Little Germany after the German Jewish industrials who built them, provided the exterior of Turton's warehouse and the interior and exterior of the police station.

In the nightclub, the men are seen dancing the Charleston and tango, which for filming was overseen by choreographer Diana Scrivener. 'The tango has featured in *Downton* before,' explains Diana, 'but we've been waiting years to include the Charleston, which up until now wasn't in vogue. By 1927, however, it was taking the country by storm as it was such an exciting and liberating dance. For Thomas's introduction to an illegal nightclub, the Charleston worked perfectly.

'To rehearse the scene,' continues Diana, 'I had previously auditioned some of the background dancers in Leeds, and I then did a couple of sessions on set with Robert and Perry. As it's a nightclub, the dancing isn't meant to look overly polished and it all worked out really well.'

Downton's composer, John Lunn, was also on set in a cameo role, playing his own music on the piano. Composers tend not to meet cast members, but working on *Downton Abbey* has always been a very different experience for John. Nevertheless his turn in Turton's is the first time audiences will see him on film, as John explains: 'Last time I was playing the piano in *Downton* my face didn't make it into the final cut so I was pleased to see I was left in the edit this time!'

ANNA and MR BATES

Joanne Froggatt
Brendan Coyle

Anna and John Bates are in a good place right now. Happily married and with a young son, also John, they are, in the words of Joanne Froggatt, who plays Anna, 'very happy in work, in life and love'. Still working at Downton Abbey, Anna as maid to Mary and Mr Bates as valet to Robert, they have been through turbulent years. Mr Bates injured his leg in the Boer War, Anna was sexually assaulted (Joanne receiving a Golden Globe for her performance of the storyline), both have spent time in prison and yet the two have somehow managed to overcome everything.

The couple are thoroughly decent and loyal to the Crawley family. Anna is a kind and generous soul, and Mr Bates is naturally calm, patient and a little more enigmatic, and both feel lucky to have found each other. Having gone through so much adversity, they both also have an inner strength and a determination of will that comes to the fore in the movie.

In defiance of the royal servants who condescend to the Downton staff and sweep them aside, Anna and Bates decide they should take matters into their own hands. They assemble everyone in the wine cellar and take the lead in plotting against the royal household. 'There's a great clash between the well-oiled machine that is Downton Abbey,' says Brendan Coyle, who plays Mr Bates, 'and this royal "carnival" almost that comes to the house.'

'Anna has also really come into her own,' says Joanne. 'She's really taking charge of her life and then leads the way with the revolution

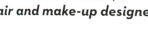

of the downstairs staff. She's also a little bit naughty in the film but on the right side of naughty in order to put people in their place. She is by no means a walkover.'

Anna's moral compass is on red alert when it emerges the Queen's dresser, Miss Lawton, has been stealing precious trinkets from the house. Rather than turn Miss Lawton in, however, Anna turns the situation to her advantage by coercing the seamstress to alter Edith's ballgown in return for Anna's silence over the stolen items and their safe return.

Over the years, Anna has developed a close bond with Mary and they often share their private thoughts in the sanctity of Mary's bedroom. 'They have always supported each other and in a way Anna mirrors what Mary is doing upstairs,' explains Joanne. 'Mary has taken on the role of being protector of Downton and the person that will take it forward. Anna is completely committed to helping Mary and does her bit in her area of the house to support Mary in that quest.'

Mary: 'You're a good friend to me, Anna.'

Anna: 'I hope we're good friends to each other, m'lady.'

Joanne was pleased to be back on set, particularly filming the bedroom scenes: 'On the first day of filming, Laura [Edith], Michelle [Mary] and I did a scene together and we couldn't believe we were back again, we were like giddy schoolgirls. In fact, coming back to the *Downton* set, having all been away doing other projects for around three years, was a bit like coming back to school after the summer holidays and being able to catch up with your friends.'

Brendan also enjoyed seeing familiar and new faces on set: 'It was great to have these new actors, like David Haig, come and hit the ground running. They've entered the world of *Downton Abbey* and shifted it a little.'

As a couple, Anna and Bates' allegiance to Downton Abbey is unwavering, and when Mary voices her concerns about whether she can really take the estate into the future, Anna tells her in no uncertain terms that Downton Abbey is the beating heart of the community and it is up to Mary to keep that heart beating. By promising her mistress that she can count on her and Mr Bates, Anna helps Mary edge towards the realisation she must do exactly that.

Behind the Scenes

THE WINE CELLAR

Anna: 'We are going to clear the way so you cook
and serve dinner for the King and Queen
at Downton Abbey. As you should.'
Mrs Patmore: 'Well, oh my God. Is this a revolution?'
Molesley: 'Should I fetch the pitchforks?'

One of the first days of filming at Shepperton was the scene where the downstairs' staff gather in the wine cellar to plot against the royal household. Fed up of being pushed aside, Anna and Mr Bates announce they all must 'defend Downton's honour' and fight back against the tyranny of the visiting servants. The majority readily join in the revolution, although Carson is deeply uncomfortable with the situation, which to him smacks of treason – 'We'll all end up in Botany Bay!' – although even he concedes that his counterpart, the Page of the Backstairs Mr Wilson, has treated him deplorably.

As the scene was early on in the shoot, many of the cast were excited to be back on the *Downton Abbey* set, albeit in the unfamiliar location of the wine cellar, one of the newly built additions at Shepperton. Kevin Doyle explains the challenge of getting back into character as Mr Molesley straight away for such a pivotal scene: 'It was great to be back but it was quite a weird morning for all of us, as we hadn't been together for three years and there we all were in this rather confined space. After such a long time away, you do have to remind yourself how your character speaks and recreate their physicality – there's no slowly getting into the swing of it.'

Raquel Cassidy, who plays Miss Baxter, also vividly remembers how the actors were feeling as they prepared for the scene, 'As it was one of the first where the downstairs cast were all together, the atmosphere was quite jovial and heady. The mood of the scene we were playing, though, was quite different, and Michael [Engler], the director, had to work a bit to get us in that place, explaining that by taking matters into our hands we could have got the sack, so the stakes were quite high for our characters. It was a great scene to play, one in which the Downton staff enter as individuals and leave almost as a little army.'

Michael remembers the cellar being a serious scene but with a comic edge. 'I wanted to find the right balance, between the stakes being real enough but doing it so it still played to the comedy of the situation. *Downton* is quite unique in that way – it has so many different characters with storylines that can be comic, political, romantic and emotional, and yet it all feels like one world. A lot of that, of course, is down to the scripts and the way Julian Fellowes writes them.'

MRS PATMORE

Lesley Nicol

We find Mrs Patmore, played by Lesley Nicol, still at the helm of the kitchen at Downton Abbey, whipping up great quantities of delicious food all through the day. The kitchen is a constant hub of activity; food is prepared and cooked from scratch, and Mrs Patmore runs her domain with formidable pride. In the past, Mrs Patmore had been resistant to new electrical gadgets in the kitchen, partly because she feared it could spell the end of her job. By now, though, she has just about got used to having a refrigerator, which is a permanent fixture of the kitchen.

In such a pressurised environment, it's no wonder that Mrs Patmore is quick to speak her mind. Lesley Nicol jokes that her character is a bit like Gordon Ramsay, as when checking a plate of food she will, 'look at it, season it and then shout at a few people!'

Tensions run particularly high when the kitchen staff learn that when the King and Queen arrive at Downton members of the royal household will take over all their duties. Mrs Patmore, who has always fought her corner, is – unsurprisingly – indignant when she is pushed aside by the superior royal chef Monsieur Courbet, with whom she has several run-ins, referring to him openly as 'Oh Mighty One'.

Monsieur Courbet ultimately gets his comeuppance, as does the Page of the Backstairs, Mr Wilson, whom Mrs Patmore 'accidentally' covers with the sticky contents of her mixing bowl. It was a scene that Lesley particularly enjoyed playing, and one that she had to get

right in the first or second take. 'Luckily, David Haig, who played Mr Wilson, was very good about it all!'

Mrs Patmore still has a strong bond with under cook Daisy, the two spending long hours in the kitchen together. While neither she nor Sophie McShera, who plays Daisy, actually make any of the food we see on screen, they are both adept at knowing exactly what they should be doing when they deliver each line, such as chopping parsley or mixing a sauce – but they do draw the line at anything too complicated.

Did making a *Downton Abbey* film feel any different for Lesley? 'Not really,' she says, 'I thought it would and I kept saying to Sophie, should we be doing things any differently? But no, we just carried on as normal and I loved every minute.'

Mrs Patmore: 'A royal luncheon, a parade and a dinner? I'm going to have to sit down.'

Behind the scenes, home economist Lisa Heathcote oversees the food seen on screen, all of which must be authentic to the period but also look good on camera and stand up to the rigours of filming. Having worked on *Downton Abbey* since the first season, Lisa draws from her knowledge of country-house fare, while also making use of period cookbooks.

Royal chef Monsieur Courbet prepares a lavish feast for the royal party upstairs, which is promptly discarded and replaced by Mrs Patmore's food when the Downton staff take over all arrangements for the grand evening meal.

To recreate the kind of food served to royals, Lisa used, among other references, cookery books by Charles Elme Francatelli, who was a popular Italian-British cook and chef to Queen Victoria. 'Much of the food prepared by a royal chef would have been quite intricate and frightfully grand,' explains Lisa. 'Jellies were really popular and they used a lot of aspic in the period – everything was set quite firmly (just like their hair!) which helped to preserve the food and show it off. Glacé fruit and sweetmeats, which were expensive to produce, would have also featured on royal household menus.'

The ill-fated feast that Monsieur Courbet prepared included a rib of beef and a game pie, which was in reality filled with porridge oats as no one was actually eating it. Lamb cutlets would also have appeared on a royal menu; Lisa's for the scene were coated in a white béchamel sauce, decorated with tarragon and glazed with aspic, then put in a pastry basket marked with crowns.

DAISY and ANDY

Sophie McShera
Michael Fox

Of all the downstairs staff, under cook Daisy is the least excited at the prospect of royalty staying at the house, declaring early on, 'I agree with Mr Branson. I don't like kings either.' 'Daisy is kind of baffled by all the excitement,' says Sophie McShera, who plays her. 'For the kitchen, visitors of any kind, in particular royal visitors, simply means more work for the staff and she can't see what the fuss is all about.' Daisy is even less impressed when she discovers that the Downton staff will play no role in the royal visit – 'I think it's rubbish. They impose, they demand, and now we're to be made nothing in our own house.'

Over the course of the *Downton* series, we've seen Daisy grow from a young girl with limited schooling into a woman in her twenties, now with some education and firm views on what she wants in life. 'Daisy has been on a bit of journey, as she always has been since the first season,' says Sophie. 'She's constantly making discoveries about how she feels about the world, how she feels about the house and the people in it. I love that about her.'

Daisy questions what the world has in store for her and dares to dream of a life outside service. She and footman Andy are now engaged, although she's not ready to discuss plans for a wedding and begins to have doubts about him. Michael Fox, who plays Andy, explains, 'Andy wants to start a life with Daisy but she's not ready to do that. She thinks Andy is quite safe and a little ordinary.'

'For Andy and the other footmen, serving the King and Queen was like playing in the FA Cup final – it was such a huge moment in their lives.'

Michael Fox

Daisy's head is turned when Tony Sellick the plumber turns up – she's impressed by his ambition and desire to do well in life, and worries that Andy lacks similar drive. Andy clocks Daisy's interest in Mr Sellick and in a fit of jealous rage damages the newly fitted pump in the boiler. This made for a memorable scene for Michael Fox, as he explains: 'I didn't expect the boiler to be quite so big – it was like the engine room in the *Titanic*! Ben Smithard [the director of photography] was lying down under the valves, waiting for me to come in with a shovel and smash it. He had to wear safety goggles as it was all a bit precarious.'

When Andy confesses to Daisy after the dinner, much to his surprise she is impressed by his evident passion: 'You risked being sacked, you risked ruin, just for the love of me?' Andy's actions serve

Daisy: 'They're all mental. All this fuss for a man and woman we don't know.'

to bring the two together, with Daisy now happier to discuss plans for marriage.

Michael was delighted to have a few significant scenes in the movie, particularly as he had expected only to be in one episode of the television series when he originally joined for the final episode of season four. 'It was great to be back on set, and as I only joined in the last two seasons, for me it all finished a little sooner than I would have liked. They are all such a great group of actors, and on the film I really savoured every moment.' Sophie was similarly happy to be back among friends, particularly her sidekick Lesley Nicol, who plays Mrs Patmore, the two characters having worked together in the kitchen for so many years.

Daisy: 'You tried to wreck the visit of the King of England. You risked being sacked, you risked ruin, just for the love of me?'

TONY SELLICK

James Cartwright

Tony Sellick, the plumber, makes quite an impression on Daisy. His energy and ambition – not to mention his film-star looks – are captivating, and he certainly rocks the boat when he arrives at Downton Abbey to fix the boiler. Like Daisy, Mr Sellick is determined to make something of his life and poor Andy feels he suffers by comparison.

James Cartwright, who plays the role, agrees: 'Tony Sellick represents that emerging working-class mentality. He's building up his business and wants to be his own boss, and Daisy admires his get-up-and-go.' Andy, of course, secretly sabotages the new pump Mr Sellick installs. 'But it has the reverse effect,' laughs James, 'as it means I have to come back to Downton!'

James loved every minute of filming *Downton Abbey* and found coming on to the set at Shepperton a wonderful, if surreal, experience: 'The set for the kitchen and all the downstairs areas is incredible. It's so real looking that it's not a huge leap of imagination to believe you're actually there in 1927.'

James admits he hit the gym prior to taking the role, just in case he was asked to take his shirt off during filming, although he soon learned that that would not have been the done thing at Downton Abbey! Regardless, Mr Sellick certainly makes his presence felt and James was simply thrilled to be part of the whole *Downton* experience, just sitting in the kitchen, enjoying a cup of tea (black, no sugar) while Mrs Patmore told him he'd done a good job with the boiler. 'It really was like being transported back in time!'

▲ Women packing Rowntree's Cocoa, York, 1929.

◄ Office workers with mechanical calculators, 1929.

▼ A Lancashire spinning shed, 1926.

Working Women

For women like Daisy, life was very different to those led by the upper classes. However, with a little education under her belt, she has the increasing confidence to question accepted values in society and dreams of a better life for herself outside service. The generation before her would probably have been only too glad to have had such a good position in a house, but with improving literacy rates and wider access to popular culture, even those living in a rural outpost of Yorkshire could see that modern life could offer more independence and excitement than their parents had experienced.

Many women were keen to work in offices, factories or shops rather than the rigidly controlled environment of service. Despite this, servants were the largest occupational group in 1927 and in 1931 there were still some 1.4 million indoor domestic servants, 1.2 million of whom were women. Nonetheless, domestic service had lost some of its sheen of respectability, and deference to one's employers had also begun to erode in the 1920s with servants increasingly viewing their work as a job rather than a life-long calling.

MR MOLESLEY and MISS BAXTER

Kevin Doyle
Raquel Cassidy

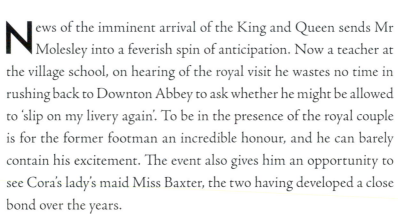

News of the imminent arrival of the King and Queen sends Mr Molesley into a feverish spin of anticipation. Now a teacher at the village school, on hearing of the royal visit he wastes no time in rushing back to Downton Abbey to ask whether he might be allowed to 'slip on my livery again'. To be in the presence of the royal couple is for the former footman an incredible honour, and he can barely contain his excitement. The event also gives him an opportunity to see Cora's lady's maid Miss Baxter, the two having developed a close bond over the years.

As a character who's always had respect for authority and status, it seems fitting that Molesley should be back at Downton Abbey, now that the very pinnacles of society are within its walls. Such is his fervour, though, that no one has the heart to tell him that the royal servants are to do the waiting . . . until the Downton servants decide to take matters into their own hands.

When Miss Baxter first learns of the royal visit, she is excited too but, unlike Molesley, keeps her composure. 'She's not running down the corridors screaming or anything,' says Raquel Cassidy, who plays her, 'but she's excited, in a very Baxter way!' Miss Baxter has something of a chequered past and is thus grateful for her job and will do all she can to keep it. Nonetheless, she does go along

Molesley: 'Do you think I might be allowed to slip on my livery again?'

with the rebellion in the servants' quarters, as Raquel explains: 'She's seen the build-up of slights from the royal servants, knows that that's not the way to behave and her sense of justice is piqued. She'd never lead this revolution – her whole livelihood depends on her job – but she's definitely up for it.'

Kevin Doyle, who plays Mr Molesley, was delighted to feature in the movie and he captured the awkward humour of his character to perfection. A key scene for Molesley is the evening dinner party, which he treats like a theatrical performance, worrying that he'll forget his 'lines' before they head upstairs. While serving, Molesley commits an atrocious faux pas by addressing the King directly, which immediately silences the room. When he recognises what he has done, Molesley is almost paralysed with humiliation,

Molesley: 'I know I'll forget my lines.'

Baxter: 'You haven't got any lines!'

Anna: 'You're on. And Mr Molesley, remember to breathe!'

performing a cringing bow crossed with a curtsey as he backs away from the table.

Kevin Doyle had earmarked the filming of that scene as an important day in his diary. 'There was a lot of anticipation about that scene and I knew I had to get it right. In fact, filming it was probably one of the scariest moments of my career!' he remembers. 'I had to make a complete idiot of myself in front of the likes of Maggie Smith [Violet], which I've obviously done before in the television series, but this was on a much grander scale and magnitude!'

The scene required Kevin to show the poor footman's dawning apprehension of his error: 'Molesley's glee turns to abject horror when he realises what a complete fool he's made of himself. The whole scene was set up brilliantly and I just focused on not messing it up.'

Once the dust has settled after the royal visit, Mr Molesley has a quiet chat with Miss Baxter and confides in her that he clearly

made a fool of himself, to which she replies that, to her, he 'could never be a fool'. It's a subtle suggestion of something more between them. Both actors were aware that some *Downton Abbey* fans were keen for something to develop between the two characters, who have often supported each other through difficult times. But as Kevin reminds us: 'These are two people who have been hurt in the past and so if anything were to happen between them, they would be cautious and take slow steps.'

The wardrobe department did a lot of research into the state liveries worn by the servants at great houses. State livery differed from house to house and was worn at formal occasions in the presence of esteemed guests, the King and Queen being the most esteemed of all. For the Downton livery, the team used the beautiful Downton green colour for the wool tailcoats, with silver braiding, and then extra detail of lacing on the cuffs, pockets and front breast and waistcoats. The royal household servants would have looked very splendid in their scarlet livery, which juxtaposed well with the green worn by the Downton staff. Both are worn with white breeches and white silk stockings. The only exceptions to this are Carson and Wilson, who are in black breeches and black stockings, matching the attire of the gentlemen.

DOWNTON STATE LIVERY

Dancing Partners

In Molesley's excitement over the royal visit, he waltzes Mrs Patmore around Mr Bakewell's shop, singing a popular tune from the period, the chorus of which includes the line: 'I've danced with a man who's danced with a girl who's danced with the Prince of Wales.'

The Prince of Wales referred to here was King George's eldest son, the future King Edward VIII, who was the subject of breathless admiration in the 1920s. The fashion editor Diana Vreeland described him as 'the Golden Prince . . . To be a woman of my generation in London – any woman – was to be in love with the Prince of Wales.' One of the most eligible bachelors in the world, women clamoured to dance with him, and those who had could become famous overnight. In the US, the term 'dancing partner' became a euphemism for his mistresses and a parody guide to etiquette joked that all high-society wedding parties should have at least one bridesmaid who had danced twice with the Prince.

In the song, the girl who danced with the Prince refers to Edna Deane, a world-champion ballroom dancer at the time (Fred Astaire described her in 1929 as 'authentic poetry in motion'). At a ball in the 1920s, the Prince was so entranced by Edna that he is said to have asked her to dance nine times. The incident inspired the songwriter Herbert Farjeon to pen the popular song.

▼ The Prince of Wales surrounded by women at a film premiere in 1932.

*I've danced with a man who's danced with a girl
    who's danced with the Prince of Wales.
It was simply grand, he said, 'Topping band,' and
    she said, 'Delightful, Sir.'
Glory, Glory, Alleluia! I'm the luckiest of females;
For I've danced with a man who's danced with a girl
    who's danced with the Prince of Wales.*

*My word I've had a party, my word I've had a spree.
Believe me or believe me not, it's all the same to me!
I'm wild with exultation, I'm dizzy with success,
For I've danced with a man I've danced with a man
    who –
Well, you'll never guess!*

*I've danced with a man who's danced with a girl
    who's danced with the Prince of Wales.
I'm crazy with excitement, completely off the rails,
And when he said to me what she said to him –
    the Prince remarked to her
It was simply grand, he said, 'Topping band,' and
    she said, 'Delightful, Sir.'
Glory, Glory, Alleluia! I'm the luckiest of females;
For I've danced with a man who's danced with a girl
    who's danced with the Prince of Wales.*

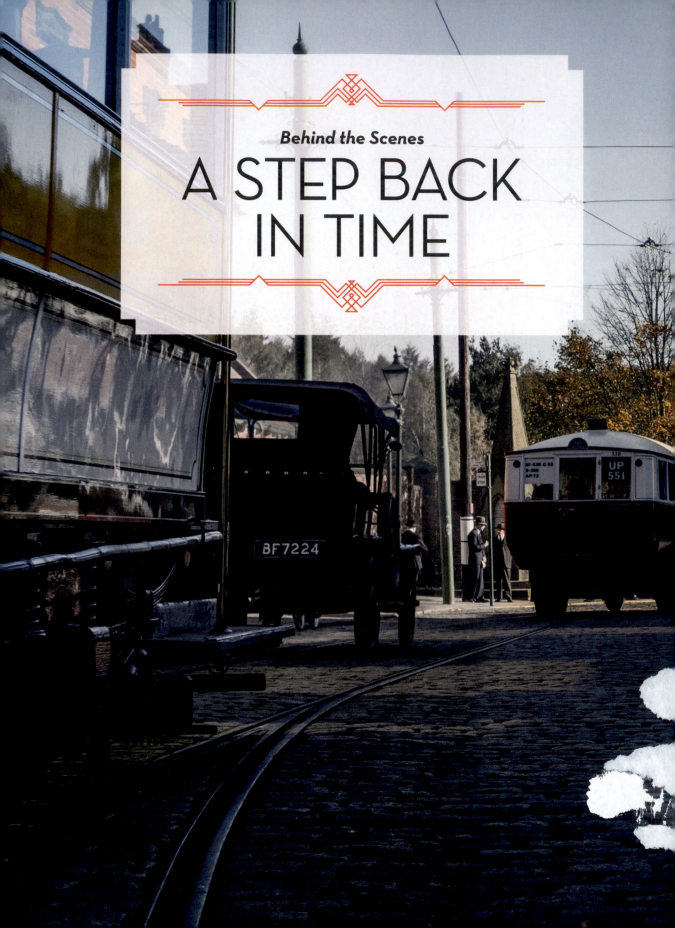

Behind the Scenes

A STEP BACK
IN TIME

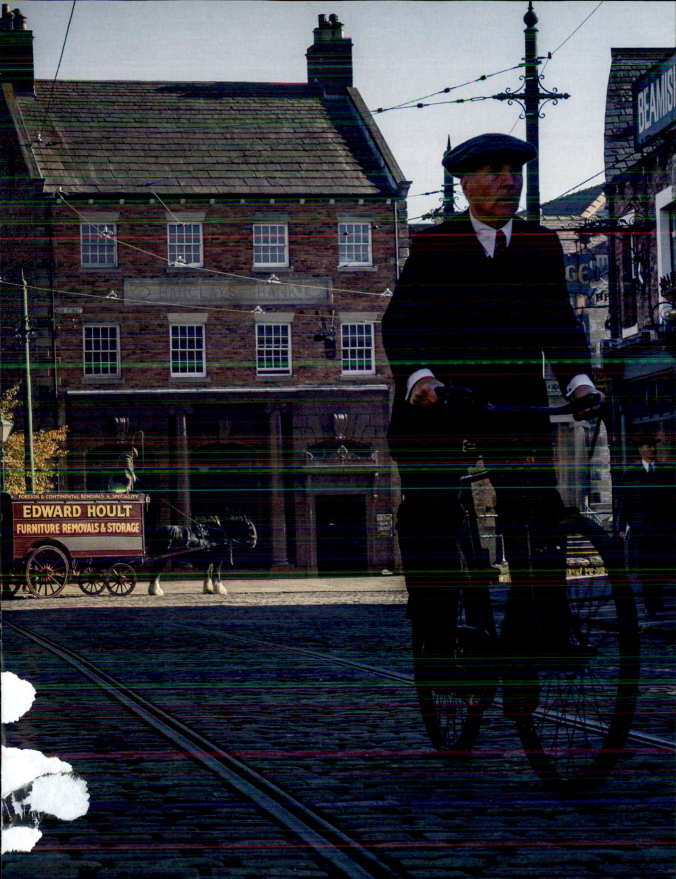

Chetwode: 'The papers tell me the King and Queen
will be staying at Downton Abbey during
their tour of Yorkshire.'

Branson: 'Well, if it's in the papers,
it must be true.'

Scenes featuring Mr Bakewell's shop and Tom and Henry's car showroom were filmed at the open air museum of Beamish, in County Durham.

Location manager Sparky Ellis explains: 'We filmed there for the television series so it was great to be back to recreate York, where Tom and Henry's car showroom is based.' For the showroom itself the film used the Beamish Motor & Cycle Works, which was built in the early 1990s as a replica of a typical garage in the early years of the twentieth century.

Beamish supplied a variety of motor and horse-drawn vehicles, as well as a bus and two trams, which ran in York between 1910 and 1935. We see two open-topped tramcars, the Newcastle 114, which has wooden seats inside for fifty-three passengers, and the Blackpool 31, originally built in 1901. The bus is a 1928 Northern SOS bus, which was painstakingly restored by the Friends of Beamish. As Sparky explains, 'We were keen to get the hustle and bustle of a busy street scene and block-booked various trams and vehicles so they would be running on time for us. We really wanted to go the extra mile for the film and fill that big screen.

For Mr Bakewell's shop, which is in the village of Downton, the crew turned their cameras away from the busy street outside to show the grocer excitedly serving Mrs Patmore and Daisy in the authentic interior, which even includes a brass till made by the National Manufacturing Company of Dayton, Ohio – the company who produced the first cash register in 1879.

'When we shot at Beamish,' recalls Sparky, 'the museum was still open to the public, although I think the visitors were quite excited to see the *Downton Abbey* crew filming there.'

MR BAKEWELL

Mark Addy

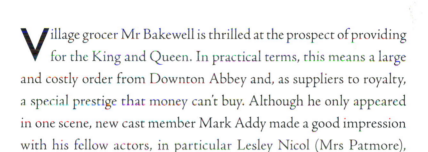

Village grocer Mr Bakewell is thrilled at the prospect of providing for the King and Queen. In practical terms, this means a large and costly order from Downton Abbey and, as suppliers to royalty, a special prestige that money can't buy. Although he only appeared in one scene, new cast member Mark Addy made a good impression with his fellow actors, in particular Lesley Nicol (Mrs Patmore), who remarked: 'Mark just seemed to get better and better with every take.'

When Mrs Patmore and Daisy head to the village to see Mr Bakewell, they are left in no doubt over the shopkeeper's enthusiasm about the royal visit. 'My heart is fit to burst, I don't mind telling you. I shall have fed the King Emperor from my own shop. If only my father were alive. He'd be so proud of me.' With an excitable Mr Molesley singing and dancing around them, Mr Bakewell adds, 'This is the peak of my career. Well, the peak of my life, really.'

In the face of such jubilation, it's no surprise that Mrs Patmore struggles to break it to him that they won't be cooking for the King and Queen. Fortunately, Daisy overrules Mrs Patmore and insists they keep the news to themselves, to avoid 'ruining Mr Bakewell's year'. At the house, Daisy then secretly takes in the order of food and hides it in a cupboard, which is just as well as all of it will eventually be used when the Downton staff stage their revolution. Thankfully, Mr Bakewell is none the wiser and we sense that he'll bask in the glory of being a supplier to royalty for many years to come.

The Royal Household

A vast retinue of servants and staff accompanied the royal family wherever they went. In the movie, we learn that teams of royal servants would arrive ahead of the King and Queen, then leave to return to them or to prepare the next location, in a military-style operation that swept all before it.

As the Downton staff look on bewildered, Mr Wilson attempts to explain how this system works: when the royal couple is on the move, there are two of each servant – two valets, two dressers, two chefs, even two groups of four footmen – with one group staying with the King and Queen while the second group goes ahead to prepare for their arrival.

In the movie, the servants shuttle between Raby Castle, a little further north in County Durham and the next destinations on the royal tour: Downton Abbey and Harewood House. They ensure that the ground is fully prepared, that every need of the royal couple is catered for, while Their Majesties bring along with them an equerry, a lady-in-waiting, two detectives and a chauffeur.

The complex relay system of servants is a true reflection of royal procedure, and one that was well rehearsed over the many tours and trips away. When Queen Mary stayed at Holker Hall in Cumbria, in 1937, it is recorded that she brought with her two dressers, one footman, a page, two chauffeurs, a lady-in-waiting, a maid for the lady-in-waiting and a detective.

Her list of requirements were sent ahead to the house: a chair to be placed outside her room for a page to sit on, fresh barley water placed in her room every two hours, and she brought with her her own bed linen.

It has been said that when the real Queen Mary visited great houses she would often spot items – such as a china plate or item of silver – that she liked and hint to the owner that she would like it 'as a gift'. They in turn would feel obliged to give it to her, and she would add it to the Royal Collection.

The Queen's demands could be viewed as fairly modest when one considers that at their own royal households there were hundreds of servants, from valets, maids, footmen, cooks and cleaners to the more senior staff of equerries, ladies-in-waiting, secretaries, clerks and minor officials. (In the Georgian royal household, there were around 950 royal servants, organised into a web of departments, from the Pages of the Backstairs and dressers to rat-catchers and 'necessary women', who emptied the chamber pots and swept the floors.)

Below stairs the order of precedent for visiting servants was just as intricate – a servant ranked on the same scale as his master or mistress and his or her place sitting at the servants' table was arranged accordingly. In the movie, the King and Queen's servants deem themselves so superior to the Downton staff that they are frankly appalled that they must even sit at the same table as them.

Jobs in the royal household were much sought after, not only because of their prestige but also because royal servants generally lived in good accommodation and were well fed. Nonetheless,

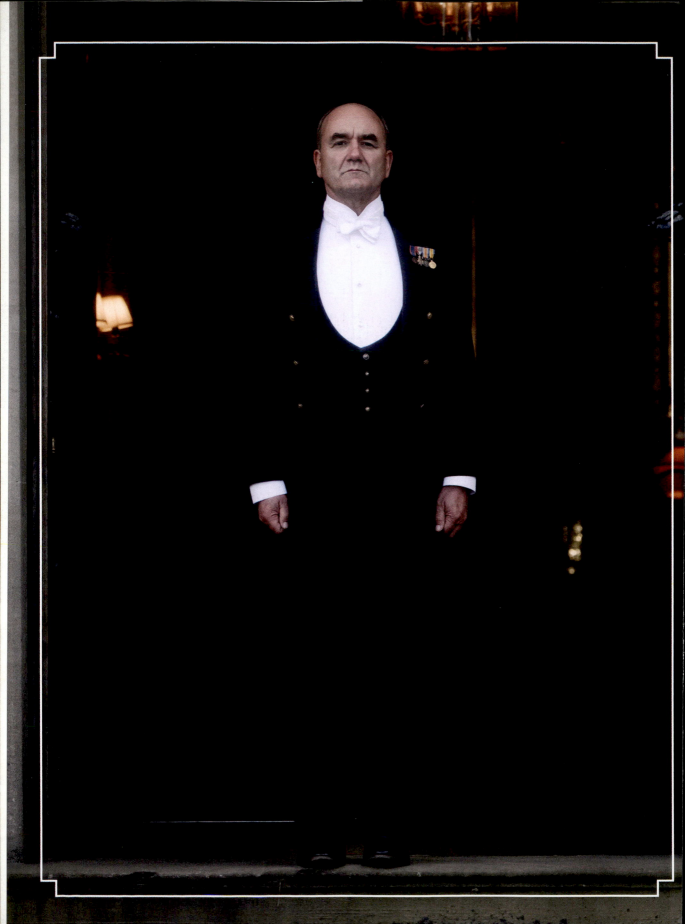

MR WILSON

David Haig

Mr Wilson leads the invasion by the royal household and immediately makes his mark as an intensely disagreeable character. The King's Page of the Backstairs is as pompous in title as he is in personality, a trait that David Haig, who plays Mr Wilson, displays brilliantly.

From the outset Mr Wilson has total disregard for the staff at Downton and takes himself very seriously, all of which causes outrage and ridicule among the Downton staff. 'Wilson's pride at being the Page of the Backstairs is inordinate,' remarks David, explaining Wilson's indignance at being called a 'butler' when he arrives and his disregard of Carson. 'As provincial butler of a house far from London, Carson would to him seem very inferior and that of course causes conflict between the two.'

Mr Wilson is unapologetic in his superior attitude, as Mr Carson discovers when he enters the butler's pantry and is surprised to find Wilson sitting at his desk, decanting wine. Without hesitation, Wilson says, 'Mr Carson, you are a retired servant in a minor, provincial house, serving an undistinguished and unimportant family.' The slight is like a physical blow to Carson and he leaves bruised from the encounter.

The Page of the Backstairs title is in a fact a real one and the current Queen Elizabeth II has four of them. They are senior servants in the royal household, attend to the Queen at all times and are the only individuals who can give others access to the private rooms of the Queen and the Duke of Edinburgh. Created by Queen Anne in the 1700s, these pages were positioned literally on the 'backstairs' which led to the monarch's private apartments. A recent well-known Page of the Backstairs was William Tallon, nicknamed 'Backstairs Billy', who devotedly served Elizabeth, the Queen Mother, for fifty-one years.

David's experience on set couldn't have been more different to that of his character – his immediate impression of filming *Downton Abbey* was how welcoming everyone was.

As his character appears both upstairs and downstairs, David also got to experience the different worlds of *Downton*, filming

at Highclere, Shepperton and the other locations that feature in the movie. Most of David's dialogue, however, was downstairs, as David explains: 'As you climb the stairs, you know you're in for long periods of silence. I think I said about six words in the first five days of filming. At Highclere, I did a lot of what Jim [Carter] has been doing for the last few years, such as serving tea very silently to the royal family and aristocrats. In fact, my biggest challenge in filming was pouring the tea with my right hand. I'm naturally left-handed, which in those days was frowned upon, so I had to swap over hands, which is quite difficult!'

In the end, the Downton staff exact their revenge on Wilson. Mrs Patmore 'accidentally' throws the contents of her mixing bowl over him and he is forced to go to his bedroom to change, but is unable to leave as he can't open his bedroom door. Of course, Andy has secretly locked it, but assures Mr Wilson afterwards that it must have stuck. David adds, 'When I read the part, I immediately thought of Shakespeare's character Malvolio, who is pompous and vain and then rightly gets his comeuppance.' David's comparison is apt: Malvolio is a proud servant in Shakespeare's comedy *Twelfth Night* who takes himself so seriously that he becomes an easy target for the other characters in the story – who eventually humiliate him. 'It's always satisfying for the audience to see someone like that tumble. The more vain and self-assured he is initially, the more fun the audience has in seeing him fall.'

Mr Wilson: 'Excuse me!
I am not a butler.
I am the King's Page
of the Backstairs.'

MRS WEBB

Richenda Carey

The alarming figure of Mrs Webb, the royal housekeeper, arrives at Downton Abbey and immediately tells Mrs Hughes, 'You are not housekeeper so long as His Majesty is under this roof!'

Mrs Webb certainly comes across as rude and overbearing, although, like Mrs Hughes, she has a job to do, as Richenda Carey, who plays her, explains: 'In the pecking order of the time, Mrs Webb was of course higher in status than Mrs Hughes and she can't understand why the Downton staff are trying to subvert everything and get in their way. What I think people also tend to forget,' continues Richenda, 'is that people really needed to keep their jobs. There was a lot of insecurity below stairs and Mrs Webb wants to get on with her job, and she feels she's being prevented from doing that. She's trying to impose some order on this chaotic household and I think gets very frustrated that she can't.'

Nevertheless, our sympathies are firmly with Mrs Hughes and we really do feel the rage of one normally so composed. Richenda of course knew when she took the role that Mrs Hughes was a much-loved character in *Downton Abbey*, and that she would come across a 'complete devil' by trying to cross her. The scenes between the two housekeepers are predictably fierce, although Richenda herself and her experience on the *Downton* set was the opposite: 'Phyllis [Mrs Hughes] was completely adorable and lovely to me. In fact, the whole cast were incredibly welcoming and not at all 'grand'. In between takes, I could always find a semicircle of canvas chairs and have a good old gossip – it was such a treat.'

MISS LAWTON

Susan Lynch

As the Queen's dresser, Miss Lawton clearly feels she is a cut above the rest and more than worthy of her position in the royal household. Chatting with Anna and Mr Bates, she smugly informs them that she's a professional dressmaker, with a reputation that befits her lofty position at the palace.

Susan Lynch, who plays Miss Lawton, relished playing the role and from her first audition worked closely with the creative team to get a handle on the character. 'Miss Lawton really does believe she's the "chosen one" and she's clearly a very good seamstress.'

She boasts that she 'trained under Madame Lucile'. Madame Lucile was a preeminent fashion designer in the early twentieth century. Officially Lucy Christiana, Lady Duff Gordon, she worked under the professional name of Lucile (and incidentally survived the sinking of the RMS *Titanic* in 1912). From her palatial headquarters in London, she developed the first global couture brand and *Vogue* hailed her as a fashion icon, the English grande dame of Parisian glitz. Society ladies, from the actress and socialite (and former mistress of George V's father) Lillie Langtry to the queens of Spain and the more conservatively dressed Queen Mary, all clamoured for her feminine and frothy gowns. If Miss Lawton had trained with Madame Lucile, she would indeed have been a much sought-after seamstress.

Nonetheless, her grand airs don't stop Anna becoming suspicious when various items belonging to the Crawley family go missing from

Anna: '"Queen's dresser a thief!" That'll make headlines from here to Peru.'

the house. It turns out that Miss Lawton has indeed been pilfering these trinkets and Anna confronts Miss Lawton with her discovery.

'When she's caught,' says Susan, 'there's that initial moment when she genuinely believes she has the right to take the items because they mean nothing to an aristocracy who are lavished with wealth and glory, whereas she has so little relatively. At the same time, she's aware that she'd suffer absolute humiliation if people found out, but she holds real conviction in doing it – and I liked that juxtaposition of character.'

Ultimately, Miss Lawton is allowed to get away with her misdemeanour, although she is made aware just how precarious her position is. With everything returned and Edith's ballgown altered, Anna well and truly won that particular battle.

'We gave Susan Lynch an Eton crop, which is a very sharp, almost boyish hair-do and was quite different to anyone else. It worked well for her character.'

Nosh Oldham,
hair and make-up designer

MR ELLIS

Max Brown

Of the trio of royal servants who arrive at Downton ahead of the main royal party, the King's valet Richard Ellis is the most approachable. 'Unlike the others,' explains Max Brown, who plays Mr Ellis, 'he doesn't take it all so seriously. He finds the Page of the Backstairs amusing, as well as the anger of the Downton staff, and sits between the two worlds.'

In cahoots with Mr Barrow, with whom he immediately strikes up a friendship, Mr Ellis helps to dupe the other royal servants by pretending to be 'Sir Harry Barnston' on the telephone, insisting that the royal footmen come to London. As Max says, it was an interesting scene to do because 'I was pretending to be someone else playing someone else! I tried a few ridiculous voices and hopefully one of them worked.'

'Initially, the relationship with Thomas and Ellis is fairly ambiguous,' explains Max. 'Michael [Engler], the director, was keen to keep it that way and to play up the romance.'

When Thomas is arrested by the police in York, it is Mr Ellis who comes to his rescue, securing Thomas's release by showing his 'Royal Household' card. He advises Thomas to be more circumspect in future and we begin to suspect there's more to him than meets the eye. Thomas and Ellis continue to talk and the intimacy between them grows until they kiss. Mr Ellis leaves Thomas with a key ring as a memento, saying, 'It's not much, but I've had it for years. It'll remind you of me . . . So you can think of me 'til we meet again.'

MONSIEUR COURBET

Philippe Spall

Monsieur Courbet wastes no time in making his presence felt when he first arrives at Downton Abbey with housekeeper Mrs Webb and four footmen from the royal household. They are greeted by some of the Downton staff and Mr Carson points them in the direction of the servants' entrance. Monsieur Courbet, however, has other plans. 'I am Monsieur Courbet, chef to Their Majesties!' he exclaims, as he pushes past them and heads through the front door!

Like many others of the visiting royal household, Monsieur Courbet considers himself a cut above the Downton staff and is entirely dismissive of them. In the kitchen, we see him constantly haranguing and barking orders, although Mrs Patmore is less inclined to jump at his every word, remarking when he rudely asks where he should put his cooking pot, 'Don't tempt me.' Philippe Spall, who plays Monsieur Courbet, agrees. 'Most of my scenes involve raised tempers – he wants to make everything just so, and he's not the sort of person who will tolerate fools gladly.'

Clearly under immense pressure, having to move from house to house and deliver sumptuous meals for the royal party, Monsieur Courbet is nonetheless haughty and insufferable, with an air of ridiculousness about him. 'We talked about making him quite a heightened character,' explains Philippe. 'He's a Frenchman who has been living in England for a long time and in the process has taken on English aristocratic airs and graces. So he speaks with this French accent but with a particular English affectation. His

pomposity and confidence in himself and his status certainly assists in making that transition!'

Philippe, who is himself half-French, has had some experience acting around food, having once appeared in a theatre production where he had to cook a whole meal live on stage. For *Downton*, he was only required to whip the odd thing in a bowl as his character spends most of his time rushing about the kitchen telling people what to do. To add to the background noise of the servants' area, Philippe, like many of the actors, was called in after filming to record some additional dialogue, such as the line when Monsieur Courbet commands his staff to 'prepare to do battle with the barbarians'.

Like Mr Wilson, the imperious Page of the Backstairs, Monsieur Courbet receives his just comeuppance when, having prepared great piles of lavish food for upstairs, he is forced to retire to his bedroom overcome with tiredness, requesting to be woken in half an hour. Unbeknown to him, Anna has slipped a sleeping draught into his cup of tea and he will be out for the rest of the night. This allows the Downton staff to take over all preparations and serving duties for the evening dinner and Courbet misses the entire thing. At breakfast the next morning, he and Mr Wilson threaten to investigate what went on the previous night; Mr Carson advises them not to unless they 'enjoy ridicule', as Mrs Hughes has received compliments from upstairs about Mrs Patmore's food, which clearly had gone down well with the royal party.

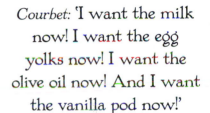

Courbet: 'I want the milk now! I want the egg yolks now! I want the olive oil now! And I want the vanilla pod now!'

Mrs Patmore: 'He wants a clip round the ear. Now.'

Courbet certainly has a distinctive look, and hair and make-up were delighted to see that Philippe had grown his hair fairly long prior to filming. 'I had this rather ridiculous coiffed, curled and primped look to go with my character,' explains Philippe, 'and to keep my curls in place I was put in a red hairnet every morning. It meant when all the ladies were being put into curlers, so was I!'

Despite the unpopularity of the chef, Philippe found the experience of being part of the *Downton Abbey* film simply joyous and his arrival at Highclere, drawing up in the 1920s 'charabanc' with the rest of the royal household staff, was a particularly memorable moment: 'It was a beautiful day, but also a little misty and just for a while it really did feel like the clocks had been turned back.'

YORKSHIRE'S GREAT ESTATES

While the film returns to Highclere, it also features a host of new locations, many of them in the beautiful county of Yorkshire, home to the fictional Downton Abbey. These include the very grand Harewood House on the outskirts of Leeds, and the ballroom of Wentworth Woodhouse, which is captured in all its glory in one of the final scenes of the film.

A key location for the *Downton Abbey* movie, and one of the grandest, was Harewood House in Yorkshire, the family seat of Princess Mary's husband, Lord Lascelles.

The use of Harewood House as a location for filming was in fact entirely appropriate to the storyline. Harewood is the family seat of the real Lascelles family. It was here that Princess Mary, Lord Lascelles and their two sons lived and she is buried at All Saints' Church, in the grounds of the estate, alongside her husband. Today it is the home of the 8th Earl of Harewood, Princess Mary's grandson.

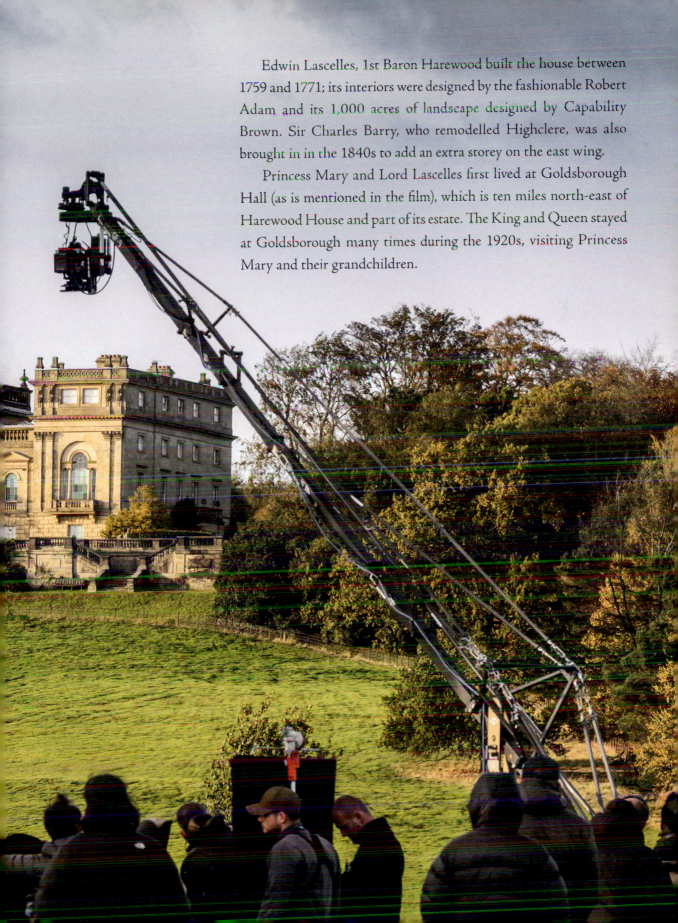

Edwin Lascelles, 1st Baron Harewood built the house between 1759 and 1771; its interiors were designed by the fashionable Robert Adam and its 1,000 acres of landscape designed by Capability Brown. Sir Charles Barry, who remodelled Highclere, was also brought in in the 1840s to add an extra storey on the east wing.

Princess Mary and Lord Lascelles first lived at Goldsborough Hall (as is mentioned in the film), which is ten miles north-east of Harewood House and part of its estate. The King and Queen stayed at Goldsborough many times during the 1920s, visiting Princess Mary and their grandchildren.

The family then moved to Harewood House in 1929, after the death of Lord Lascelles' father, and they set about modernising the house, installing twenty new bathrooms (it previously had only two) and adding a nursery on the top floor of the east wing for the boys.

Happiest in the Yorkshire countryside, Princess Mary and her family enjoyed outdoor pursuits and the boys spent a happy childhood in their thousand-acre playground. The house itself provided a splendid venue for entertaining the great and the good, with frequent shooting parties and house parties for races at nearby Wetherby and York. In the early 1930s, the large lake at Harewood froze over for three weeks. As a result, Lord Lascelles, by now 6th Earl of Harewood, arranged an ice hockey match for the family and staff, with one team led by the head gardener and with the Princess in goal.

Members of the royal family were also regular guests at Harewood and, as she had done when the family lived at Goldsborough Hall, Queen Mary spent ten days each August with her daughter on her way north to Balmoral in Scotland. In 1933, the King and Queen stayed at Harewood House during a trip to visit Leeds, where they opened the Civic Hall. As they travelled through the city, a large crowd of people from all over Yorkshire turned up for the royal procession from the suburb of Oakwood to the Civic Hall and then the Town Hall where, in a similar event to the parade in the movie, the King inspected the guard of honour.

Today, the royal family are still regular visitors at Harewood and the property is often open to the public. The house impressed both cast and crew, some of whom had visited before, including location manager Sparky Ellis: 'It is a beautiful house and we did actually consider Harewood prior to the first season when we were scouting for locations for Downton Abbey itself. Of course, we went for Highclere in the end, but it was great to be back there.'

The protocol surrounding hats was fairly rigid at the time and removing them could be something of an undertaking, particularly if a lady's maid was not on hand to help. When Edith suggests that it won't be necessary for Violet to change for the buffet dinner but will just need to take off her hat, Violet is suitably aghast at the proposition: 'You talk as if that were easy.'

The convention of the time was that if a woman made a visit to another house, she would not take her hat off, but if she received guests in her own house she would. So, when Cora, Edith and Mary visit Princess Mary at Harewood, they keep their hats on while Princess Mary does not. It was much simpler for men whose hats would come on or off as they left or entered houses.

In 1927 cloche hats continued to be all the rage, although women still wore wide-brimmed hats too. In the movie Anna Robbins dressed Mary and Edith in cloche hats, which worked well with their shingle bob haircuts, while Isobel and Cora wear wider brims to give great drama and presence.

PRINCESS MARY

Kate Phillips

We first meet Princess Mary, the daughter of King George and Queen Mary, at Harewood House. Here she receives Cora, Mary and Edith for tea and amid the opulent surroundings of the house we also get a first glimpse of the Princess's husband, Lord Lascelles, and their two young sons.

As Princess Mary lives fairly locally, the Downton set are obviously used to seeing her at various functions in the county, and prior to this event, there has been some discussion about how sad the Princess often seems. Isobel remarks on this, although Violet sees her demeanour as fitting for someone of her station, replying, 'She is royal. Royal women are not meant to grin like Cheshire cats.'

Royal or not, there is certainly a sense of melancholy about Princess Mary, which Kate Phillips, who plays her, was interested to explore. 'In the script, she comes across initially as quite sad and she does have a shy temperament. Of course, the royal family were quite burdened by this overall sense of duty, and there were episodes in Princess Mary's life where she really stepped up to the mark, doing a lot of charity work during the war. So she was pretty robust but reserved at the same time.'

'During the film,' Kate continues, 'she's allowed to overcome her shyness and she shines more – and I think Michael [Engler, the director], was keen to draw that out and show a different side to her. In fact, I had an opportunity to talk to Michael about the character of Princess Mary – on the surface she's very controlled and rehearsed but inwardly there's this world of emotion. We talked

about what's buzzing underneath, which really helped me to flesh out the character.'

Contributing to Princess Mary's sadness is her apparently strained relationship with her stern husband, Lord Lascelles, played by Andrew Havill. He fails to accompany the Princess at various events, as noticed with increasing concern by the King and Queen, and frowns upon the appearance of the children during tea, although the two boys are clearly a source of delight to Princess Mary.

In playing a royal, Kate was also intrigued to talk to historical advisor Alastair Bruce, who briefed her on how she should hold herself, which she found invaluable in creating the outer shell of her character, while everything else was bubbling below the surface. 'Changing your posture or mannerisms really affect the overall rhythm. I'm quite jittery in how I speak and use lots of hand movement, which is something she wouldn't have done. There was

a scene with Branson, when he comes upon me when I'm lost in my thoughts, and I turn. I instinctively turned very quickly, as that's just me, and Michael had to remind me to turn more slowly and sedately.'

That scene with Tom Branson, where the two characters talk alone in the grounds of Downton Abbey, was a key one for Kate. Branson notices that something is troubling Princess Mary, although he doesn't know who she is. Recognising this, she grabs the opportunity to have a frank conversation with Branson, asking him how he manages to live with a family who are very different to

'Princess Mary has to straddle playing the role of princess, and what's expected of her, with her own private struggles, and there's real tension between those two things.'

**Michael Engler,
director**

283

him. 'Branson is completely open with her,' explains Kate, 'because he doesn't realise she's a princess. It's a rare moment for her – they're just two people talking – and it makes for a touching scene.'

It's an emotional moment for Princess Mary, which was helped by the fact that the scene was shot in the grounds of Highclere. 'We were sitting on a bench and I had this incredible view of rolling hills and a stunning landscape,' says Kate. 'Mary is meant to be lost in thought when Branson comes across her and the location did really help to stir up those emotions!'

The discussion has a considerable impact on the Princess — she sees that Branson has had to prioritise what's important to him and his daughter, and she in her way must do the same. In her case, she must focus on the interests that she and her husband share and make the best of it. What matters is her duty to the royal family. 'Her personal relationships have to come second to the Crown,' adds Kate, 'and that's a journey she has to go through. Her mother, Queen Mary, is already there, she just has to realise it for herself.'

The Real Princess Mary

Princess Mary, Countess of Harewood, was born in 1897, the third child and only daughter of King George V and Queen Mary. She had four brothers, the future King Edward VIII and King George VI and two younger brothers, John, who died in 1919, and George, Duke of Kent, who would die in an air crash in 1942.

The young princess grew up in York Cottage on the Sandringham estate and was tutored at home. Unlike her brothers, she showed an aptitude for her studies, becoming fluent in German and French and also developing a passion for riding. As the girl of the family, she was treated more leniently than her brothers by her disciplinarian father. The five children saw little of their father

▲ Princess Mary in 1917.

▼ Princess Mary in a Red Cross nurse's uniform with her mother.

when they were very young while Queen Mary tended to treat them as small adults and, as was typical with noble families, set aside just an hour a day to see her children (Lord Lascelles in the film was clearly brought up to expect the same).

Often isolated at home, without the company of girls of her own age, Princess Mary was reserved in public – the Prime Minister Herbert Asquith described her 'shy, girlish charm, which leaves one with the impression of nervous pleasure and fatherly respect'.

The outbreak of the First World War, however, would help to bring the Princess out of her shell. Keen to do something for the war effort, she supported her mother in public appearances and set up various projects to bring comfort to British servicemen and their families. One such

THE ROYAL WEDDING.

PHOTO. VANDYK, LTD. LADY D. GORDON-LENNOX. LADY E. BOWES-LYON. LADY MARY CAMBRIDGE. PRINCESS MAUD. VISCOUNT LASCELLES. PRINCESS MARY. MAJOR SIR VICTOR MACKENZIE. LADY D. BRIDGEMAN. LADY MAY CAMBRIDGE. LADY RACHEL CAVENDISH. LADY MARY THYNNE. 532. W. BEAGLES' POSTCARDS

▲ The ceremony was the first to be featured in *Vogue* magazine, Princess Mary sharing details of her dress, trousseau and honeymoon lodgings with the readers as 'another act of friendliness to the women of the Empire'. Among the bridesmaids was Lady Elizabeth Bowes-Lyon (later Queen Elizabeth, the Queen Mother), who was a friend of Princess Mary.

project was the organisation of a fund to cover the sending of a brass tin containing tobacco, chocolates and cigarettes to every soldier fighting in France at Christmas 1914. She also supported various voluntary and charitable organisations and worked as a trainee nurse at Great Ormond Street Hospital.

Once the war was over, it was time to find Mary a husband, although it was not a particularly easy task to find a good match for a royal on British shores. In 1921, Princess Mary was seen with Henry, Viscount Lascelles at the Chatsworth estate in Derbyshire and at the Grand National horse race. Henry was the eldest son of the 5th Earl of Harewood, had a large personal fortune, vast

lands, an impressive war record, a fine collection of paintings, and shared the royals' love of shooting and riding.

The match was thus encouraged by Mary's parents although he was fifteen years older than the Princess, lacking in charm, with the look, some said, of a 'dismal bloodhound'. The stern demeanour perhaps belied a more colourful youth, as just a decade earlier he was said to have fallen madly in love with the famed novelist and poet Vita Sackville-West, whose later lovers included Virginia Woolf and Violet Keppel. In fact, it is said that Virginia Woolf based one of her *Orlando* characters, Archduke Harry, on Lord Lascelles – a comic character who is madly in love with Orlando; she finds him essentially boring and lacking in wit.

The wedding of Princess Mary and Lord Lascelles went ahead on 28 February 1922, and it was far from a quiet affair. It was the first grand state occasion since the war, and was met with huge fanfare. Royal weddings had previously been private affairs whereas this took place on the streets of London – the Princess's older brother the Duke of York remarking, 'It is no longer Mary's wedding, but (this from the papers) it is the "Abbey Wedding" or the "Royal Wedding", or the "National Wedding", or even the "People's Wedding". Pathé News filmed the grand procession between Buckingham Palace and Westminster Abbey, large crowds thronging the streets.

The newly-weds based themselves largely at the family home of Harewood House and at Goldsborough Hall on the Harewood estate. They also had residences in London and Ireland but Mary felt most at home in Yorkshire, in the relative isolation of the countryside. Two sons arrived swiftly, first George in 1923 and then Gerald in 1924. Princess Mary's shy and sometimes sad demeanour fuelled rumours that her marriage was not altogether a happy one. Lascelles appeared gruff and autocratic, not unnoticed by the royal family with Mary's eldest brother, the Prince of Wales, once commenting: 'I get commoner and commoner, while Lascelles gets more and more royal.'

In 1932, Princess Mary was awarded the title of Princess Royal following the death of her aunt Princess Louise. Lord Lascelles had succeeded his father, becoming the 6th Earl of Harewood, some three years earlier. Mary continued to make regular appearances in public, spending as much time as she could with her family in Yorkshire. She maintained a close relationship with her eldest brother, the Prince of Wales, before and after he abdicated the throne in 1936. As the Second World War broke out, she stepped up her public engagements, visiting amongst others, units of the Women's Royal Army Corps as the Controller Commandant. In 1947, Lord Lascelles died, and the Princess Royal continued to live at Harewood House with her son George and his

▲ Princess Mary with her sons Gerald and George.

family. She was made Chancellor of the University of Leeds in 1948, the first woman to hold such an office in Britain, and throughout the 1950s and 1960s, she continued to carry out official duties at home and abroad.

On 28 March 1965, while walking with her eldest son in the grounds of Harewood, Princess Mary suffered a heart attack and died in his arms. The subsequent *Times* obituary remarked upon her as someone who had an 'active, unobtrusive and personal life', who had managed to overcome her 'natural reserve' and served the nation, especially in Yorkshire where she was 'dearly loved with a constant and rare fidelity.'

LORD LASCELLES

Andrew Havill

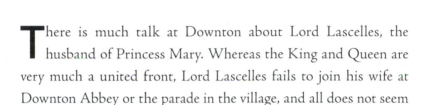

There is much talk at Downton about Lord Lascelles, the husband of Princess Mary. Whereas the King and Queen are very much a united front, Lord Lascelles fails to join his wife at Downton Abbey or the parade in the village, and all does not seem well with the marriage.

We first see Lord Lascelles when Cora, Edith and Mary are having tea with Princess Mary at Harewood. He appears at the doorway, an older, stern-looking figure who is disgruntled to see his two young sons with the ladies, as the rules of the house dictate that they're not allowed in the drawing room before six o'clock. Rather reluctantly, he acknowledges the presence of the Crawleys, stipulates that the children are not allowed at the parade as 'they'll only cause a ruckus', and abruptly departs, leaving a distinctly unfavourable impression on all present.

Andrew Havill, who plays Lord Lascelles, agrees: 'He's not a barrel of laughs and I suspect he was not much fun to be married to. He obviously likes his rules, being a military man, and he expects his family to live by them. Of course, he was involved in heavy fighting during the war and my suspicion is there was quite a lot of psychological damage there. This was very much a time of just getting on with it, stiff upper lip and all that.'

The scene where we first see Lord Lascelles was filmed at Harewood House, where the real Lord Lascelles grew up and lived with Princess Mary and the house is still the home to the current

8th Earl of Harewood, David Lascelles. In fact, there are a number of portraits of Henry Lascelles dotted around the house and the current family were delighted to see how similar Andrew looked to the real man.

For the ballroom scene, Andrew was required to wear court dress, which he had reservations about – 'I felt a bit better when I saw Matthew Goode [Henry Talbot] dressed in the breeches and stockings because he actually looked okay. However, Matthew looked far better than I did, and I remember Hugh [Lord Grantham] joking, who in history ever decided this was a good look?!'

At the ball, there is something of a truce between Princess Mary and Lord Lascelles – he asks her what she wants and she says that they need to try harder to be friends and to share the things they have in common, such as their boys and horses. In reality, the couple did make a go of it and the marriage survived, their eldest son even commenting in his memoirs that they got on well 'and had a lot of friends and interests in common'.

Princess Mary: 'I want us
to be friends.'
Lascelles: 'Well. We'll have to see.'
Princess Mary: 'No, dear. We'll
have to change. Both of us.'

Behind the Scenes

THE BALL AT HAREWOOD

INT. BALLROOM. NIGHT.

The first dance is finishing. Lord Lascelles is with the Queen, the Princess with her father. But now they return to their spouses. It is a waltz. Gradually couples join, including Mary and Henry, Edith and Bertie, Robert and Cora.

The stately home of Wentworth Woodhouse provided a suitably grand backdrop for the ballroom scene in the movie. Filming of the dancing took place in the stunning Marble Saloon, where in history some of the house's most extravagant balls have been held, with royal guests at some. With its high stucco ceilings and grand proportions, the saloon could also accommodate a large production crew and equipment, an orchestra and space for the key cast and extras to dance.

For the director of photography Ben Smithard and the whole crew, it was a challenging scene to film. 'It's a big space and there were a lot of cast and extras involved. One of the cameras was on a crane shooting the main dance below – the camera would travel around in one direction and then the opposite direction, changing the background and isolating different characters as they danced. This helps to add dynamism and allows the editing team to choose the right shots for the scene.'

The cast enjoyed filming the grand ball scene, although it was a long and exhausting day for many of them. Douglas Reith, who plays Lord Merton, recalls, 'It was a huge dancefloor and we were all dressed in our finery. The men were in court dress:

tail coats, white waistcoats and white tie, breeches, tights and patent pumps. Most of us knew how to waltz but we had to do the Viennese waltz which is really fast. It involves spinning around and around and it's very easy to get dizzy and you really have to whoosh your partner around with each turn – good fun but demanding.'

The scene also featured professional musicians in the orchestra, who had to mime playing their instruments. The dancers had the music playing through earpieces – not unlike a silent disco – so the cast's microphones could pick up their dialogue.

To prepare for the ballroom scene, dancing rehearsals were of course a must. These were overseen by choreographer Diana Scrivener, who had worked with the cast and crew of *Downton Abbey* for many years. Prior to the shoot, she had one day of rehearsals, which took place at the London Academy of Music and Dramatic Arts (LAMDA). In the morning, she worked with her 'core' dancers: six couples made up of ex-LAMDA students who would be dancing near to the main cast. She then went through the steps with the actors, making sure they felt comfortable with

the technique, while her core dancers moved around them. 'If any actors then try speaking their lines and it somehow doesn't fit or they don't feel comfortable, then we might adapt things a little,' explains Diana. 'With dialogue, the camera is going to be focused on the upper part of the body and not on their feet. So if they need to move slightly less when speaking, that's fine, and then they can get back to the set piece.'

'You often have dialogue in dance scenes, as there's intimacy between the couples. In the past, so much happened at dances and these scenes provide film screenwriters with the perfect means to get across an important point. What they might not realise is the total fear many actors feel when they know they have to walk and talk at the same time!'

For the actual dances, Diana chose firstly to do the veleta, although we only see the very end of that dance in the ballroom scene. 'It was a popular, beautiful dance, involving couples moving around the ballroom all doing the same thing, like a formation dance,' explains Diana. 'As the King

and Queen, and Princess Mary and Lord Lascelles were dancing, we wanted something that was regal and not too fast. After that, the main dance we see is the Viennese waltz, in which couples move around and around, with lots of movement and gives the impression of real activity.'

For filming, Diana recruited a few more people to be background dancers and oversaw all the dancing during the two days they were shooting in the magnificent ballroom of Wentworth

Protocol dictated that only married women could wear a tiara. As Isobel, Edith and Mary are now all married, Anna Robbins was able to give them all tiaras in the movie. The ones worn by Violet, Cora and Edith at the ball were all authentic diamond tiaras on loan from London jewellers Bentley & Skinner.

In the script, Edith's ballgown is made by Madame Handley-Seymour, a real-life upmarket atelier who was known for reworking catwalk looks in her London salon, so Anna Robbins looked to Parisian designs as reference. 'I wanted to put Edith in gold, to create a dress that had great dramatic effect. I sourced a panné velvet from Italy, which draped beautifully with lovely movement, and commissioned a print for the velvet to add a metallic shimmer.'

The shooting schedule meant that Anna first had to make the over-sized shapeless version of the gown that Edith receives by mistake, and then transform the same dress to fit Laura Carmichael – exactly as Miss Lawton has to do in the film.

Woodhouse. Filming usually involves lots of takes and the dancers were required to repeat the action again and again. 'As the day progresses people get tired,' says Diana, 'but they also get better as they get used to what they're doing, especially if they're getting positive comments from the director.'

On a personal note, Diana was delighted to see that almost the final scene of the *Downton Abbey* film was one that included dancing: 'Having worked on almost all of the television series, it was the icing on the cake really, and the fact that I was involved was very special.'

AFTER THE FILMING

Once the ten weeks of filming was finished and the grounds of Highclere, Harewood and the other locations were finally clear of the travelling circus of trailers that accompany all film units, the process of post-production could begin. Over a period of several weeks, director Michael Engler and film editor Mark Day worked closely in the cutting room to create the critical 'director's cut' of the movie. Together they went through every scene, editing out lines, reordering, adjusting or removing scenes all together. Their aim was to achieve just the right pace, excitement and emotion, whilst fitting all the action within the film's eventual running time of two hours.

Mark (with his assistants Sascha and Thy) had in fact been working on the movie since day one of filming (and for a week or two before in preparation). After each day of shooting, 'rushes' (or 'dailies' as they are called in the US) are sent through to the editor in the cutting room who starts to put together a scene, gradually building up the scenes as the shoot progresses. Each scene is shot from a number of angles, varying from wide or mid-shots to over-the-shoulder takes focusing on the actors' faces. There are many different shots for each scene, and each may require multiple takes, for example if an actor makes a mistake or the director wants a different performance.

Consequently Mark received a great deal of footage each day, all of which he had to sort through to assemble each scene. On set, Michael and the producers also looked at rushes every day and checked with the cutting room that they had everything they needed. 'If, for example, we had

only two days left of filming at Highclere,' explains producer Liz Trubridge, 'Michael might check to see if he needs to pick up on anything else.'

Once filming was over, Mark could go through his initial cut with Michael: 'At this stage, it will be a much longer version of the film as I always include all the scenes in script order, as that's what the director has had in mind during the shoot,' explains Mark. 'But I'll have in my head scenes that can be cut or restructured. I might be wrong and the director might want something entirely different for a scene – it's all part of the process, and things change and evolve over the many weeks that we work together.' The aim of the director's cut is to make the most of every scene and every performance. If it's an emotional scene, such as the one between Violet and Mary at the end of the film, the edit should convey that sentiment, hit just the right pathos, whilst remaining true to the characters. Similarly, the final ballroom montage was a crucial scene as it will be the last time audiences see many of the key characters so the aim of the edit was to capture the wonderful looks and performances of each couple dancing.

Once Michael and Mark had worked through everything and had a cut they were happy with, they then showed it to the producers, Gareth and Liz, as well as Julian Fellowes, who passed on their own notes and ideas. When Focus Features had also given their approval on the cut, the film was shown to test audiences both in the UK and US. For movies, this is standard practice, but it's not such a regular occurrence for television productions, so this was a first for *Downton Abbey*.

At each screening, around 250 cinemagoers watched the film and some of the production team sat in with them. 'You can pick up a lot from the audience's body language,' explains Mark, 'whether or not they shuffle around and how they respond to seeing characters for the first time or to certain moments in the film.' Audience members filled out a questionnaire and focus groups talked about various issues, such as areas they didn't understand, or characters they liked and disliked. The feedback from these test screenings often proves invaluable and following this there may be the decision to shoot another scene or two. A couple of scenes were added to the *Downton* movie: Branson's conversation with Major Chetwode in the village pub, which helped to clarify their storyline, and a scene that emphasised the antagonism between Mr Carson and Mr Wilson.

Once the new scenes had been slotted in and all the executives involved were happy with the cut, the film edit was 'locked' and the real post-production process kicked in. This involves the 'spotting' of various elements, from visuals effects to sound and music. For *Downton*, visual effects mainly involve removing any signs of modernity, such as spotlights, alarms or vapour trails in the skies from overhead planes. In the movie, grass was also made to look a little more pristine, particularly after the hot, dry summer of 2018 when it was shot, and rural Pickering Station was transformed to recreate King's Cross Station.

With the visual effects in place, Ben Smithard and the film's colourist Gareth Spensley can 'grade' the film – balancing the colours and illumination of the movie, adjusting its contrasts, hues and textures, all of which adds to the atmosphere and famously rich feel of *Downton Abbey*.

Vital also to *Downton Abbey* is its audio, its sumptuous music score and the sound effects and design, which serve to underpin the drama and

storytelling of the movie. Emmy-award winning composer John Lunn, who wrote the original title track and worked on the entire television series, similarly composed the music for the film. 'We knew we wanted to retain many of *Downton*'s original themes in the movie, because it's so integral to the show and is familiar to the fans. That was really brought home to us when we had a test screening of the movie in Los Angeles – as soon as the title music came on, the audience started cheering and tearing up. So the essence of the title music is very much the same but it's now on a grander scale, and recorded by a bigger orchestra.'

From the outset, the music transports us to the world of *Downton Abbey*, as familiar chords and a pulsating rhythm accompany the visuals on screen as the letter wends its way to the house. 'The opening music should give you a flavour of the journey you're about to go on,' adds John, and in fact the first five minutes of the movie are entirely

filled with music, which builds to the moment when the camera finally pans up to Downton Abbey; the chords open out and we are treated to the full splendour of the title music.

John first wrote the music on a keyboard, matching all the action and sequence of scenes from the final edit of the film. A team then helped to orchestrate and record his compositions, which were played by a seventy-five-piece orchestra and John on the piano.

Once John had created the music for the movie, the show's re-recording mixer Nigel Heath blended it together with the sound effects and dialogue to create the finished soundtrack. This building process starts with the dialogue track recorded using radio and boom mikes during filming. The sound crew normally do such a good job that very little needs to be re-recorded but sometimes actors are required to re-do the odd bit of dialogue – known as automated dialogue replacement (ADR) – if there's an intrusive noise in the background, or the producers have requested a slight amendment to a line in the script.

During this ADR process, some of the actors were also asked to provide background voices, as Nigel explains: 'Downton has a large ensemble cast so for big scenes, such as the dinner party, we need the actors to provide background chat, in order to create an authentic soundscape.' This chatter shouldn't, however, detract from any key dialogue in the scene. 'We make sure the principal dialogue is razor-sharp and then we smudge and defocus the background dialogue so the audience is steered to the key action.'

At this stage, other sounds that can't be captured during filming are added, all of which gives extra depth and realism to the movie. In a purpose-built studio known as a 'Foley stage' specialist performers create authentic sounds to synchronise with the action on screen. For example, for Carson's footsteps they always use the same pair of shoes (so even if we can't see him on screen, we know it's him) but the stage is adapted to different floor surfaces, from gravel to a sprung ballroom. Similarly, the Foley artists always use the same prop to create the familiar sound of Violet banging her stick on the floor. Occasionally the sound crew on location will capture a specific sound effect on a 'wild track' when the camera isn't running, as they did at Highclere when they recorded Andy winding the clock.

This layering of sounds, along with crashes and noises coming from other rooms, creates the effect that Downton Abbey is a busy and active house. 'We wanted the house to feel alive, so when you're in the servants dining area, you might also be able to hear the kitchen or corridor off-screen,' explains Nigel, 'Similarly if someone drops a real bombshell of a line, you can cut the background noise to create more impact and drama.' This technique was used to good effect when the Downton servants plot their revolution – once the wine cellar door was shut all background sound was taken away, heightening the atmosphere.

Upstairs, the sounds are a little different, you might hear birdsong or a clock ticking. There's an illusion of space and air, whereas in the servants' quarters the sounds add to the feeling of claustrophobia and heat. The noises used for Carson's garden give a real feeling of being outdoors and you can almost smell the flowers. For a movie this immersive feeling could also be enhanced with the use of Dolby Atmos surround sound so that when, for example, Mr Barrow walks down into Turton's nightclub cinema audiences initially hear the hubbub in front of them, but when he enters, it comes from all around.

All these layers are then blended together to form the film's soundtrack, which is married to the pictures before being packaged into a digital format under the guidance of post-production supervisor Ann Lynch.

And the final film is complete. For the first time in its history, Downton Abbey will be shown in cinemas across the world. After years of planning, a project that has been a labour of love for so many people, the Downton Abbey film is finally here. The doors to the great house will open once again to receive guests.

WELCOME TO DOWNTON ABBEY – WE'VE BEEN EXPECTING YOU.

First published in the United States by St. Martin's Press, an imprint of St. Martin's Publishing Group.

Text copyright © 2019 Focus Features LLC. Licensed by Universal Studios. All Rights Reserved.

Printed in the United States of America.
For information, address St. Martin's Publishing Group, 120 Broadway, New York, NY 10271.

www.stmartins.com

FOCUS FEATURES A COMCAST COMPANY **CARNIVAL**

Original photography by Jaap Buitendijk with additional photography by Liam Daniel © 2019 Focus Features LLC

Costume sketches by Anna Robbins © 2019 Focus Features LLC

Buckingham Palace Royal Arms © Crown copyright

Designed by Dan Newman at Perfect Bound Ltd

The Library of Congress Cataloging-in-Publication Data is available upon request.

ISBN 978-1-250-25662-1 (hardcover)

ISBN 978-1-250-25661-4 (ebook)

Our books may be purchased in bulk for promotional, educational, or business use. Please contact your local bookseller or the Macmillan Corporate and Premium Sales Department at 800-221-7945, extension 5442, or by email at MacmillanSpecialMarkets@macmillan.com.

Originally published in Great Britain by Headline Publishing Group, an Hachette UK company

First U.S. Edition: September 2019

10 9 8 7 6 5 4 3 2 1

Archive Photography credits
Bettmann/Getty Images 77tl; Borthwick Institute/Heritage Images/Getty Images 229tr; Central Press/Getty Images 157tl; Donaldson Collection/Getty Images 77tr; Fox Photos/Hulton Archive/Getty Images 238; FPG/Hulton Archive/Getty Images 173tl; George Grantham Bain Collection, Library of Congress Prints & Photographs Division: 141, 143, 145, 286; Hulton-Deutsch/CORBIS/Corbis via Getty Images 229mr; Hulton-Deutsch Collection/CORBIS/Corbis via Getty Images 173tr; SSPL/Getty Images 229tl; Topical Press Agency/Getty Images 157br; Universal History Archive/Universal Images Group via Getty Images 138; W & D Downey/Hulton Archive/Getty Images 140.

Select Bibliography
Catherine Bailey, *Black Diamonds: The Rise and Fall of an English Dynasty*. London: Penguin Books, 2007.
David Cannadine, *George V*. London: Penguin Books, 2014.
Jessica Fellowes, *The World of Downton Abbey*. London: HarperCollins, 2011.
James Pope-Hennessy and Hugo Vickers, *The Quest for Queen Mary*. London: Hodder & Stoughton, 2018.
Kenneth O. Morgan, *The Oxford Illustrated History of Britain*. Oxford: Oxford University Press, 1984.
Jeremy Musson, *Up and Down Stairs: The History of the Country House Servant*. London: John Murray, 2010.
Ted Powell, *King Edward VIII: An American Life*. Oxford: Oxford University Press, 2018.
Emma Rowley, *Behind the Scenes at Downton Abbey*. London: HarperCollins, 2013.
Adrian Tinniswood, *The Long Weekend*. London: Vintage, 2018.
Adrian Tinniswood, *Behind the Throne*. London: Jonathan Cape, 2018.
John Van Der Kiste, *George V's Children*. Stroud: The History Press, 1991.

Acknowledgements
It has been a real pleasure and a privilege to enter the world of Downton Abbey and to meet and talk to the extraordinarily talented and dedicated cast and crew involved. My thanks to Gareth Neame and Julian Fellowes for giving me their time and granting me access to their remarkable creation. Thank you also to Liz Trubridge, Michael Engler, Mark Hubbard and all the *Downton Abbey* crew who have generously spared time out of their busy schedules to talk to me, particularly Anna Robbins, Anne 'Nosh' Oldham, Mark Day, Lisa Heathcote, Donal Woods, Ben Smithard, John Lunn, Nigel Heath, Jill Trevellick, Mark 'Sparky' Ellis, Ann Lynch, Diana Scrivener, Gina Cromwell and Kimberley Bright. A huge thank you also to Charlotte Fay who essentially made this book happen, and was immensely efficient, helpful and cheering throughout. Many thanks also to all the *Downton Abbey* cast who gave me their time and insights into filming – it has been a real honour.

At Headline, many thanks to Sarah Emsley and Katie Packer for their dedication and support. And thanks also to the supremo-editorial and design team Emma Tait and Dan Newman, for their sterling work, support and friendship over the (very many) years.